The Healthy Christian Life

The Healthy Christian Life

THE MINIRTH-MEIER CLINIC BIBLE STUDY GUIDE

FRANK MINIRTH, PAUL MEIER,
RICHARD MEIER and DON HAWKINS

BAKER BOOK HOUSE 
Grand Rapids, Michigan 49516

ISBN: 0-8010-6232-2

Eighth printing, May 1993

Printed in the United States of America

Contents

Introduction

The Minirth-Meier Clinic is committed to a Christian ministry that involves integrating Scripture with the professional counseling process. The authors, with a combined experience of more than sixty years in pastoral or clinical ministry, are committed not only to Scripture's inerrancy—its complete truth—but to the application of its timeless principles into the three major areas of life—physical, emotional/psychological, and spiritual—in order to produce healthier and more complete individuals.

One of the most powerful tools available to help maintain a healthy Christian life is Scripture memory, especially when combined with Scripture meditation. Memorized verses can serve as an instant reference when help is needed with various problems. Some tips that have helped many Christians through the years in memorizing Scripture are:

1. *Enjoy Scripture memory.* You tend to continue doing the things you enjoy most. If you memorize verses that build, protect, and meet specific needs in your life, then you will enjoy the process of memorization more than if you just memorize random verses. It is helpful to choose verses that cover the basics of Christian living (for example, salvation, fellowship, and so on) along with other specific areas of need, such as depression, anxiety, or loneliness.
2. *Carry Bible memory cards.* It is helpful to make or buy small Bible memory cards to carry with you throughout the day to aid in your memorization and scriptural meditation.
3. *Share memorized verses with others*—family members, friends, those in need. This really helps to reinforce the content of the verses in your own life.
4. *Pray the verses back to God.* Having a conversation with the Lord about what he has said is also effective.
5. *Circle memorized verses in your Bible.* This will enable you to

make a special effort to go over them again when you are reading through that portion of text.

You are especially encouraged to memorize Scripture verses that relate to your specific spiritual and psychological needs. Suggested verses dealing with particular emotional problems are listed on page 9. Many of them are also used as the memory passages assigned to each chapter in this book.

We believe you will find that the use of this Bible-study series can uniquely promote spiritual, physical, and mental well-being as we progress together toward the goal of becoming balanced and healthier servants of God.

For further information regarding the nationwide services of the Minirth-Meier Clinic, please call

1-800-545-1819

Bible Verses Dealing with . . .

1. *Getting to Know God*—John 3:16; 1:12; Romans 3:23; 6:23; Acts 4:12; Ephesians 2:8–9.

2. *Assurance of Salvation*—John 10:27–30; 3:16–18; 1:12; 6:35–37; 1 John 5:11–13.

3. *Assurance of God's Forgiveness*—1 John 1:9; Psalm 103:12–14; 32:1–5.

4. *Assurance of Answered Prayer*—1 John 5:14; John 14:13–14; 16:24; Jeremiah 33:3; Matthew 7:7–8.

5. *Marriage Conflicts*—Ephesians 5:22–23; Colossians 3:18–19; 1 Peter 3:1–7; 1 Corinthians 7:1–5.

6. *Parent-Child Conflicts*—Deuteronomy 6:4–9; Ephesians 6:1–4; Colossians 3:20–21; Proverbs 13:24; 29:15.

7. *Loneliness*—Hebrews 13:5; Matthew 28:19; Exodus 33:7; Psalms 139:1–6.

8. *Anger*—Ephesians 4:26–27; Leviticus 19:17–18; Romans 12:15–16; Proverbs 15:1; 19:11; Ecclesiastes 7:9; Colossians 3:8; Matthew 5:21–24.

9. *Bitterness*—Hebrews 13:12; Ephesians 4:31; Acts 8:23; Proverbs 14:10.

10. *Forgiving Others*—Ephesians 4:31; 2 Corinthians 2:7; Luke 6:37; Matthew 6:14–15; Mark 11:25.

11. *Overcoming Depression*—Psalms 42:5, 11; 43:5; Genesis 4:6–7; John 14:1.

12. *Anxiety*—John 14:27; Philippians 4:6–8; Matthew 6:25–34; Psalms 27:1; 27:14; 34:4; 56:3.

13. *Trials*—James 1:2–5; 1 Peter 1:6–7; Job 23:10; Romans 5:1–5; Philippians 1:27; 1 Peter 4:12–19.

14. *Suffering*—2 Corinthians 4:17–18; 1:3–4; 12:7–10; Hebrews 12:5–11; Romans 8:28–29; 5:15; John 9:1–3; Mark 5:21–42; 1 Peter 1:3–9.

15. *Temptation*—Proverbs 4:12; 8:36; 1 Corinthians 10:12–13; Hebrews 4:15–16; James 1:13–16; Galatians 6:1.

16. *Lust of the Flesh*—Job 31:1; Matthew 5:27–28; 2 Timothy 2:22; 1 Corinthians 6:13; 1 John 2:15–17; 1 Peter 2:11.

17. *Lust of the Eyes* (Materialism)—1 Timothy 6:6–11, 17–19; Philippians 4:10–13; 1 John 2:15–17.

18. *Pride of Life*—Proverbs 8:13; 13:10; 21:24; 28:25; 1 John 2:15–17; Matthew 20:25–28.

19. *God's View of Us*—Psalm 139; Ephesians 1:3–7; Romans 8:31–39; 1 Corinthians 12:20–25.

20. *Growth in Christ*
    General—2 Peter 3:18.
    Word of God—Psalm 1:1–6; 1 Peter 2:1–2; 2 Timothy 3:16–17; Jeremiah 15:16.
    Prayer—Luke 18:1; Matthew 7:7–8; 1 John 5:14–15.
    Witnessing—Romans 1:16; 1 Peter 3:15.
    Fellowship—1 John 1:1–5; Hebrews 10:24–25.

PART 1

Growing Spiritually

The first section of this manual focuses on fundamental elements of spiritual growth. As Christian counselors, we know and have seen the importance of building a systematic basis to Christian faith to become healthier in all aspects of life.

This section covers elementary Bible-study issues such as God's love for us, the assurance of salvation, the assurance of answered prayer, the Trinity, and the Bible as God's inspired Word. It also features special keys to further spiritual growth such as having a daily quiet time, holding family devotions, and meditating on and memorizing Scripture. Practical issues such as selecting a local church and the building of a Christian support system are also addressed. In addition, this section includes studies on common areas of spiritual struggle such as resisting temptation—specifically the lust of the flesh, the lust of the eyes, and the pride of life.

Once we have trusted Christ, our ultimate goal is to become healthier Christians—more like Christ. The process of growing spiritually establishes a solid framework for all other facets of a healthy life. This is why Peter instructs his readers to "grow in the grace and knowledge of our Lord and Savior Jesus Christ . . ." (2 Peter 3:18). With this process underway, we also can begin to mature emotionally, to grow in relationships, and to correct or help others to correct any special mental and physical disorders. These are the outward evidences that we are indeed becoming healthier Christians—more like Christ.

God Loves You

1

Memorize: John 3:16, 1 John 4:9

Psychological studies indicate that one of the greatest human needs is to be loved. Just as this is observable on the human level, its truth in the God-man relationship is both basic and beyond question.

We know that God loves us because he created man "in his own image." Here we mean more than physical appearance, since man was created like God in several ways—with a moral likeness, a social likeness, and an eternal likeness. This also means that the first human had a built-in sense of right and wrong and a desire for fellowship. Furthermore, man was created to live as long as God lives—forever. Adam and Eve were created as good people, with an inherent capacity to enjoy God's love, acceptance, and care as well as an ability to feel important. These beautiful capacities were exercised as God fellowshiped with them when he came to walk with them in the cool of the day in the Garden of Eden.

Man was allowed to develop character by exercising a choice between good and evil. Adam and Eve made a bad choice when they sinned against the Creator, thus separating the human race from God. Everyone born into the world since that time is born separated from God, with an inner *sin nature.* When individuals become old enough to exercise a *choice,* they usually choose to rebel against God's will and go their own way in attitudes and behavior.

Just as an apple tree is an apple tree whether or not you see apples on it, every person is a sinner regardless of his or her outward refinement, culture, or deportment. We all start out as sinners—unresponsive to God and with unfulfilled needs for love, acceptance, care, and purpose in life. Yet God still loves his creation and has never become totally frustrated because of mankind's sin. There certainly has been a conflict between his *love,* which desires us for fellowship with him both now and in eternity, and his holiness, which cannot accept our sin without demanding a penalty for it.

God's love-inspired plan solved the problem by sending his Son to earth to die for our sins. Thus, the Lord Jesus Christ—who *is* God, the second person of the Trinity—became man and voluntarily took the responsibility for our sins on himself, dying as our substitute on the cross so that we could be unconditionally accepted by God. Christ arose on the third day with his mission fully accomplished, having paid for our sins in full. Now God in his love offers us eternal life, forgiveness of sins, unconditional acceptance, and a home in heaven. All this is provided as a free gift to any individual who will accept God's salvation by faith.

Salvation is a free gift to us because Jesus already paid for it. It is thus an error to believe we must earn God's love and acceptance by our good works, resolutions, or religious ceremonies. Faith is the method whereby we link ourselves to the value of Christ's death. Our faith must be placed solely in the person and work of Christ, trusting him alone as our personal Savior and welcoming him into our lives. Have you put your faith in Christ? If you are not sure, you may want to offer this prayer to God:

> Dear Lord, I come to you admitting I am a sinner and believing that you died on the cross to pay for all my sins. I trust you now as my Savior. I claim your forgiveness and eternal acceptance of me, as you promised in the Bible to those who trust in your Son. Amen.

If you have trusted Christ as your Savior, now or at some previous time in the past, it is reassuring to know that God loves you with a love you did not earn and therefore cannot ever lose, now that he has made you his child for eternity. God accepts you "in the beloved," which means because of the merits of Christ. This constitutes unconditional acceptance. God has transferred your guilt and condemnation back to the cross, where it was taken care of once and for all. God will never again bring up your sins for discussion or as a threat to your eternal destiny. He has come to live in your body as represented by the third person of the Trinity, the Holy Spirit. He wants to develop you to become progressively more like Jesus in your inward qualities. God loves you as much as he loves his Son, the Lord Jesus Christ. He looks upon you as someone to be treasured, as worthwhile and precious to him.

Scriptures for Study

1. *1 John 4:10.* How far did God go in demonstrating his love for us?
2. *Galatians 2:20b.* Is it proper to personalize Christ's love?
3. *Romans 5:12.* From whom did we inherit our sin nature and spiritually separated state from God?
4. *Romans 3:23.* Are we personally responsible for our sins?
5. *Ephesians 2:1.* How does Paul describe our condition before we are saved?
6. *John 6:44.* Since we have come to Christ in faith, who was really working behind the scenes to make it all possible?
7. *Isaiah 53:5–6.* Explain how you see the concept of substitution in these verses.
8. *Ephesians 2:8–9.* Explain "grace" by other words used in these verses.
9. *Romans 10:9.* What are the two key verbs that describe faith?
10. *Romans 10:13.* Faith can be expressed in a form described in this verse. What manner is suggested here?
11. *John 1:12.* What are the results of receiving and believing?

Additional Study

Read Luke 19:1–10 and see what you can discover about Zacchaeus's character.

1. Explain Zacchaeus's lost condition.
2. At what point did Zacchaeus actually trust Christ?
3. List the evidences that show Zacchaeus really did trust Christ.
4. Explain the contrast between Zacchaeus and the rich young ruler (Matt. 19:16–22).

Personal Project

In his *Systematic Theology,* Lewis Sperry Chafer has listed thirty-three things that occur when we trust Christ as Savior. See how many you can list, based on this chapter. Then see how many you can link with an appropriate verse of Scripture by preparing a chart of the events that occur at salvation. On the left side of the chart list the "Event," on the right side, add the Scripture verse.
Samples: Redemption—Ephesians 1:7; Justification—Romans 3:24.

Assurance of Salvation

2

Memorize: John 1:12; 1 John 5:11b–12

How can you know you are really saved and possess eternal life?

It is not uncommon for individuals who have genuinely trusted Christ as their Savior to have some struggles with doubts about whether or not their relationship with Christ was ever real or is still in place. Some people have a harder time with assurance than others because of the environment in which they were raised. If one's background included an alcoholic father, for example, or some type of rejection, abandonment, or abuse from a parent or other authority figure, it is more difficult to feel secure at all times, even in one's relationship with God. Again, at times there may be a struggle between our feelings and what God promises in his Word about our salvation. We must choose to accept God's Word as the highest authority for truth in our lives.

There are two ways to develop assurance and peace about the reality of your salvation. One way is through *external* evidences. You can verify that you are the child of certain parents by checking the legal document called your birth certificate. That is external evidence. Two of us served for many years as pastors and, in the course of these ministries, performed many weddings. Often, after the ceremony, while congratulating the couple as they stood in the reception line, we would ask them, "Do you feel married?" Sometimes the reply would simply be "No." Or "We are too excited to feel anything yet." We would then smile as we handed them their marriage license and say, "Here is the legal document. Believe it. You really are married, whether or not you feel it."

The legal document for the believer in Christ is the Word of God. Memorize several easy promises about being saved. Some of the best-loved ones are: John 1:12, John 3:16, Romans 10:13, 1 John 5:13. These verses describe what God promised to do for you the instant you trusted Christ to become your personal Savior. Believe this. Take God at his Word, trusting in his promises even if your feelings give you messages to the contrary. If God says it and Jesus did it on the cross—and you believe it—that settles the matter. When doubts arise, quote to yourself one of those verses you will have memorized.

There are also *internal* evidences that begin to show in the life of one who is saved. There is a new hunger for learning more about Christ from the Word. A newborn baby has inherent needs which are built-in signs of life. One is a natural hunger for milk. Believers sense a hunger for the milk of the Word. Another sign is an inner drawing toward fellowshiping with other Christians. We feel many things in common with the brothers and sisters of our spiritual family.

Further internal evidence of salvation is that we have a new nature within us, one that wants to live right and honor Christ as the purpose for our life. We can still sin, however, even though we are believers. We still have that sin nature within us that has the capacity to think evil thoughts and yield to temptation. But when believers sin, they don't need to start all over and ask Christ to come into their lives again. Once you have trusted him to come in, he will never leave you or forsake you.

But the fact remains that sin grieves the Lord. When we sin, we need to simply confess our sins to him, and he instantly forgives us. Even though we can sin, our new nature will continually hunger for doing right, and that will be our general pattern and style of life.

The following are some common questions that certain Christians with "obsessive-compulsive" personality traits tend to have regarding their salvation. An overly obsessive-compulsive personality is characterized by excessive concern about conformity and adherence to standards of *conscience.* Such individuals may be rigid, overinhibited, overconscientious, overdutiful, indecisive, perfectionistic, and unable to relax easily. For all of the doubts listed below, we have included what we consider to be appropriate responses.

1. *I fear I have not believed enough.* In response to this, the primary issue is not the amount of faith but the object of faith. A man who came to Jesus once said, "I do believe; help me overcome my unbelief" (Mark 9:24). Jesus' response to this man demonstrates that it is not the amount of faith but the object of faith that matters.

2. *I fear I am not committed enough.* In response to this, we point out that strictly speaking no one has ever been totally committed to anything, nor has anyone totally committed every area of his life to Christ. Ephesians 2:8–9 points out that salvation is a gift—one that cannot be earned and is not deserved. Titus 3:5 adds that salvation is apart from any righteous deeds we do.

3. *I fear I did not repent enough.* God never intended for repentance to be considered as a separate work apart from God's simple plan of salvation by faith. Over two hundred times in the New Testament, belief in Christ is listed as the sole requirement for salvation. The term *repentance* simply means a change of heart or mind. Once you view yourself as a hopeless sinner unable to save yourself and trust that Christ's death on the cross was payment to satisfy your sins, then your attitude has truly changed—you have repented.

4. *I did not pray enough.* There is no place in Scripture where we are told to pray a certain amount or to "pray through" in order to be saved. Obviously, to trust Christ (or as John 1:12 puts it, to have "received him") may be done through prayer. However, throughout Scripture the key term used is to *trust* Christ, not to pray.

5. *I fear I need to make restitution before God can accept me.* Obviously, many of us may feel this way. However, the key question is whether God said that this must be done. Furthermore, can a person who is not a Christian, who does not have the power of Christ within, ever do enough in the way of restitution to please God? Philippians 2:12–13 points out that we are to "work out" our salvation (the inference is that this happens *after* we have received it), for it is God who works in us both to will and to do of his good pleasure. After Zacchaeus trusted Christ, he made restitution, but not before (Luke 19:8–9).

6. *I have not been baptized.* Baptism, like many other activities, including church membership, is important for the believer. Scripture instructs us to be baptized as an evidence or testimony of our faith. However, though baptism is expected of believers, it is not specified in the more than two hundred passages of Scripture that clearly list the condition for salvation. Furthermore, every passage in which baptism may seem to be required can be properly interpreted by understanding baptism as an evidence or testimony of salvation rather than a requirement.

I know I am saved. How do I know? I have some promises from God's Word that say so. Also, I can sense new things happening in my heart and life that show me that the Lord lives within me.

Scriptures for Study

1. *1 John 5:13.* According to this verse, being assured of having eternal life was based on information given in what external form?

2. *Romans 10:13.* What does God's Word promise will happen to us the very instant we call on the Lord for salvation?

3. *John 5:24.* What promises are ours if we have heard God's Word about Christ and have believed him by acting on it in faith?

4. *John 10:28.* What words give security to the believer in this verse?

5. *1 Peter 2:2.* What internal evidence of life does both a baby and a new believer have?

6. *1 John 3:14.* What other internal change develops in the life of the real Christian?

7. *Hebrews 7:25.* For how long does Christ save us, and what is one of the guarantees that this is so?

Personal Project

Factors that might cause people to doubt salvation	***Response based on verses listed under "Scriptures for Study"***

Additional Study

John 10:27–31 provides one of the strongest statements for the security of the believer.

1. List all the reasons Jesus gives for feeling secure in our relationship with God.
2. See if you can figure out what kind of people have the right to feel secure, based on this passage of Scripture.
3. What is Jesus saying here about evidences for salvation?

3

Assurance of Answered Prayer

Memorize: John 14:13; 1 John 5:14–15

There is no comparison between the power of a pilot's right arm and the power of the massive jet engines that are placed into operation when the pilot pushes forward the controlling throttles. Likewise, there is no comparison between human strength and that of our all-powerful God. Yet, in many ways, God has chosen to link his power to our prayers. Jesus said, "If you ask . . . I will do." We could also take that promise to imply, "If you don't ask, I may not do it."

We find it easy at times to blame God for difficult-to-understand conditions in both the world at large and our personal lives. But perhaps a more realistic outlook would be that God has placed the throttles to a large extent in our hands. He has assured us—his believing people—that his strength is made available through prayer, for our own needs and those of others for whom we intercede. God will always answer our prayers, though his response may not always be exactly what we anticipated.

Who will take praying seriously? Will you? A necessary condition for effective praying is called "abiding in Christ." For a believer, this phrase can be defined as living in obedience and fellowship with God. Some conditions for abiding on a day-to-day basis are:

1. Confession of sins (1 John 1:9; Ps. 66:18). When we confess sin, we accept God's immediate forgiveness and we forgive ourselves. We stop putting ourselves down, stop brooding over the past, forget it—and move on (Phil. 3:13).
2. Obedience to God's Word as we understand it (Ps. 28:9).
3. A clear conscience toward others (Matt. 6:12; 1 Peter 3:7).
4. Freedom from purely selfish motives (James 4:2–3).
5. An attitude of trust and dependence on God in every circumstance and for every need of our life and service (John 15:5; Romans 8:28; Phil. 4:13).

The emphasis the Lord Jesus placed on praying is an example and inspiration to us. After full days and evenings of active ministry, he still got up early to pray. Jesus taught his disciples a basic plan for praying, and these principles are meant for us as well:

1. Normally we address our prayers to God, our heavenly Father. The only mediator we need between God and ourselves is our Savior, the God-man, the Lord Jesus Christ. His death on the cross paid for our sins and gives us immediate access to the Father. We never need to pray to some other person already in heaven, as if we expected that person to have a better inside track to God than we do.
2. There is no special posture required for prayer or any object we need to use in prayer.
3. Our prayers should be in the name of Jesus. As we close our prayers, we could say something like this: "I pray these things in Jesus' name, Amen." This means you are praying with dependence on your identification with Christ as your Savior, which is your claim of access to God's throne of grace. You must also believe you have his approval for what you are praying, and that the fulfillment of your prayers would honor and glorify him.
4. We can pray any time: day or evening, during times of calm or trouble. We can pray any place: privately or publicly.

A simple acrostic may help you remember the ingredients of effective prayer:

A doration of God (Rev. 4:10–11)

C onfession of any sins (Dan. 9:4–15)

T hanksgiving (1 Thess. 5:18)

S upplication: asking for specific needs (Matt. 7:7–8)

What burdens has God placed on your heart—for others or even in your own life? Push forward on the throttle of prayer and draw forth God's mighty power, which he has linked to your praying and faith. "If you ask, I will do," said Jesus.

Scriptures for Study

1. *John 14:13–14.* What is a necessary step if God is to do certain things?

2. *John 15:7.* What is a condition for getting answers to prayer?
3. *John 15:10.* What is a condition for abiding?
4. *Matthew 6:12.* Identify another preparation before asking forgiveness from God.
5. *Psalm 66:18.* What is the block to answered prayer? How do you define it?
6. *John 16:23.* What was the Lord's general plan for praying from that time on for the disciples?
7. *Revelation 4:10–11.* What words or phrases of this prayer express adoration, worship, or praise to God?
8. *Mark 1:35.* How would you describe the importance and pattern of prayer to the Lord Jesus Christ?

Personal Projects

1. Plan a personal prayer list. First, list the items for which you intend to pray. Then record the date when you began praying, the Bible verse(s) you claim as a basis for praying, and the date and way in which the prayer was answered. (Develop a chart for this.)
2. Examine Philippians 4:6 carefully. List the specific words used for prayer. Look these up in a Bible dictionary to find out exactly what they mean in this context. Keep a log for a week to determine whether or not you are using these elements in your prayer life.

How to Gain Meaning in Life

4

Memorize: Matthew 6:33; Romans 12:1–2

One of the beautiful benefits of being a real Christian is that the believer has an opportunity to find meaning and purpose in his or her life. There are some logical steps to take in this wonderful adventure of discovery.

First, as Christians we need to recognize that we have been bought with the price of the blood of Christ and therefore are no longer our own (1 Cor. 6:19–20). We belong to God. Have you acknowledged that truth to God? Christ is Lord. He is the Boss and has the right to run our lives. He is to be recognized as first in our lives, not only in a decisive act of dedication but in daily living. In fact, he is our purpose for living each day.

Second, we need to dedicate our lives, whatever we are and whatever we can be, to God. We present our bodies—our total personhood—to God as a living sacrifice (Rom. 12:1–2). A sacrifice is something valuable you give up without any plan of taking it back. It involves praying like this: "Dear Lord, I give you my life as a living sacrifice. I sign my name on the check in advance and will let you fill in the rest of your will for my life as you choose in the days ahead. I want to do whatever you want me to do with my life."

Third, we begin to search out who we are on the inside as believers. We are *ambassadors* for Christ, representing him to the unsaved people with whom we come into contact. As individuals, we are the *light* of the world for Jesus and are to help people find Christ. Each of us is the *salt* of the earth. Our presence among people ought to flavor the atmosphere for good and for Jesus' sake. Our lifestyle, along with our testimony in words, will make an impact on others for God. We have spiritual gifts that the Holy Spirit within us wants to use for expressing God's love in a special way to others.

One plan for discovering your spiritual gifts is by getting involved in a local Bible-teaching church. What kind of Christian service do you enjoy doing? Teaching? Giving manual and practical help? Organizing a group? Giving personal encouragement? Taking part in the music program? Witnessing? Shepherding? In which areas of Christian service do you see benefits and fruit? In what ways do other believers say you are a blessing to them?

Finally, we take a good look at the external circumstances of our lives. What areas of opportunity are open to you now in the area of occupation? Housewife, construction worker, salesperson, administrator, banker, pastor, social worker, something else? How can you best express through your occupation who you really are in your internal vocation or calling for God? Can you allow your light, salt, and ambassadorship for Christ to flow effectively through your occupation?

When occupational choices arise in the future, ask yourself if your goals can be more than merely material. Can they be spiritual? Can you take some training to develop your talents and skills so you can be more effective in the occupation that best fits who you are on the inside? Would some vocational testing enlarge your knowledge of your capabilities and interests?

The apostle Paul was a tentmaker by occupation, but an ambassador for Christ by vocational calling from God. He often put the two together. At other times Paul was a prisoner by occupation, but a prisoner for the Lord by vocation. He used his prison time to witness for Christ and to write letters to believers to encourage them in the Lord.

Sometimes your life may seem boxed in like a prison. You may see your opportunities as limited. That is when you must be more like the apostle Paul and make the best of a present situation as a servant of God, living to please him.

The time is likely to come when things will open up for you. God often allows us to go through some special training experiences that will prepare us to be more effective when the door of opportunity opens in the future. For believers, purpose and meaning in life is recognizing that we are not our own, but instead we belong to Christ. He is Lord and in first place in all we think and do. Have you dedicated your life to him for whatever he wills? You will then discover your calling and internal identity as God's servant and ambassador and look for ever-increasing occupational opportunities that will allow you the most freedom in expressing who you are for the glory of God. When the reward time comes in heaven, what will the Lord say were the most meaningful projects and goals in *your* life?

Scriptures for Study

1. *Romans 12:1–2.* What is the important step requested of believers if they would like to know what the good, acceptable, and perfect will of God is for them?

2. *Philippians 2:12.* How did the apostle Paul describe his basic direction in life?

3. *1 Corinthians 10:31.* What is to be the believer's ultimate goal in whatever he does?

4. *Matthew 6:33.* In lining up our priorities in life, what comes first?

5. *Acts 18:3* and *1 Corinthians 1:1.* Compare these two verses. While Paul was at Corinth, what was his occupation and what was his vocation?

6. List below some words that describe who believers are on the inside that should be expressed on the outside.
2 Corinthians 5:20:
Matthew 5:13:
Matthew 5:16:
Acts 1:8:
2 Corinthians 3:2–3:

Additional Study

1. Survey the life of Moses in the Book of Exodus. Examine his commitment of dedication to God (Heb. 11:25–27).

2. Note the opportunities Moses had to serve God. From reading the Book of Exodus, determine what specific occupations Moses had at different times. List the circumstances and Scripture references that apply:
Prince in Egypt:
Scripture:
Shepherd in the desert:
Scripture:
Leader of the nation:
Scripture:

3. When called by God to fulfill a specific service as the leader in Israel, Moses gave several reasons for not wanting to represent God. We often adopt some of these same reasons. Examine carefully Exodus 3 and 4. Find Moses' questions and God's answers.

Verse	Moses' Questions	God's Answers
3:11		
3:13		
4:1		
4:10		
4:13		

God's Word

5

Memorize: 2 Timothy 3:16–17; 2 Peter 2:21

Do you realize that when you hold your Bible in your hand, you are holding God's miracle book? The Bible is a supernatural revelation. It is God's love letter to you. It is the only communication from God to man in this world today that is inerrant (without error) and inspired by God.

What does "inspiration" of the Bible mean? It was the process in which the Holy Spirit superintended chosen human authors to compose and record without error God's revelation to man. The Spirit used the authors' individual personalities, yet through this process the words of the original manuscripts were inscribed without error. Furthermore, down through history God has preserved and protected this book so that it would be accurately transmitted to us today.

The Bible stands complete in its sixty-six books. It is given to us to teach us truth, to warn us when we do wrong, to correct us so we can overcome our failures, and to prepare us to do good things that please God and that help us to become more mature in our spiritual lives.

Why should we trust in the Bible as God's Word? One reason is because of its many fulfilled prophecies, events that were predicted in advance and have already come true to the last detail. One of the ways God separated his truth from what the false teachers presented was by proving he could foretell the future with one hundred percent accuracy. False religions could not do this. There are other so-called scriptures in the world today, but they differ from the Bible in that they lack detailed prophecies that can be verified. The Bible, for instance, foretold over three hundred separate details about the first coming of Christ. Many of its prophecies are yet to be fulfilled, especially concerning the second coming of Christ. These also will be fulfilled in God's timing.

Another reason to trust the Bible is because of what the Lord Jesus Christ said about it. He rebuked his own disciples when they were slow to believe the Scriptures. Jesus said to his Father, "Sanctify them by the truth; your word is truth" (John 17:17). He prayed that believers would be progressively set apart to God and become more dedicated to him. The tool for doing this task would be God's truth. Truth replaces the wrong concepts and messages we have picked up through the years from various sources, including the devil. But what is truth? Where is God's truth? The Lord Jesus said that *God's Word is truth.*

Another reason to trust the Bible is because of its own claims for itself. There are 3,808 times just in the Old Testament in which the Scriptures claim to come from God. In the New Testament, the apostle Paul said to certain people to whom he had ministered, "And we also thank God continually because, when you received the word of God, which you heard from us, you accepted it not as the word of men, but as it actually is, the word of God . . ." (1 Thess. 2:13). If doubters want to say the Bible is not the Word of God, then the burden of proof is on them to prove it is not. They cannot do so.

Another reason to trust the Bible is because of its power to change lives. Many millions of people in our own generation can testify to the change that has taken place in their lives since receiving the Word of God, especially the saving message of Christ. Can you agree with the apostle Peter that your being a born-again Christian is the result of responding to the Word of God?—"For you have been born again . . . through the living and enduring word of God" (1 Peter 1:23).

The Bible is the Word of God. It is inspired of God and was given without error. God's love letter to you tells the truth, especially about God and his Son. It also tells you about yourself—where you came from, why you are here, how to face your trials and testings, what God's promises are, and what God has planned for you in the future.

Devote yourself to reading the Bible, studying it, memorizing it, and meditating on it. Most important of all, apply God's Word to your personal life.

Scriptures for Study

1. *2 Timothy 3:16–17.* Identify the purposes for the Scriptures, as indicated in these verses.

2. *Zechariah 7:12.* A process is described by which God's words come to man—even those who harden their hearts against the

words. Can you identify the source of the words and the steps in the process?

3. *Deuteronomy 18:21–22.* What was a test that marked out a false prophet's words?

4. *John 17:17.* What did the Lord Jesus Christ identify as the source of truth for us?

5. *Romans 10:17.* What does the apostle Paul identify as the source of true faith?

6. *1 Peter 1:23–25.* What phrases in these verses describe the value of God's Word for us in our generation?

Additional Study

In studying the Bible we need to consider:

1. The words and what they mean
2. The grammar—the relationship between the words
3. The context—the material before or after the specific passage being studied
4. The cultural and historical background of the passage

The process of Bible study involves several steps. We should examine scriptural passages with the following questions in mind:

1. *Observation.* What does the passage actually say? This is a step often overlooked by those who would study Scripture.
2. *Interpretation.* What does the passage mean? This involves how the people to whom the passage was spoken or written understood what was being said.
3. *Application.* How does the passage relate to you? Is there a promise to claim or command to follow? This involves what the Bible means to *you.*
4. *Correlation.* How does this relate to other passages of Scripture? List passages that correspond.

Use the process outlined above to study these Scriptures:

Joshua 1:9

Observation ______________________________

Interpretation

Application

Correlation

2 Timothy 3:14–4:2

Observation

Interpretation

Application

Correlation

Daily Quiet Time

6

Memorize: Psalm 1:1–2; Psalm 119:165

Do you ever feel excited and eager to meet someone for lunch or for some other fellowship time together? Do you know that God feels that way about spending time communicating with you? The Lord Jesus said that the Father responds to true worshipers who worship him in spirit and in truth by actually seeking such people to be his worshipers (John 4:23). God actually looks forward to the times we take from our daily routine to find a quiet moment and place to let him talk to us through his Word and for us to talk to him in prayer. We also worship him by thanking him and praising him for who he is and what he means to us.

Why not make it a habit to have a special date or rendezvous with the Lord every day? Pick out some special place to meet him. It might be in your bedroom first thing in the morning or the last thing when you go to bed at night. You could choose a quiet place in the kitchen after breakfast or a peaceful room where you can eat your lunch and spend some time with the Lord. This time in quiet communion with him will make the difference in your activities and relationships during the rest of the day. We can think better when we feed on the Word. We are transformed by the renewing of our minds. We live not by bread alone but by every word that proceeds from the mouth of God.

Old Testament believers often worshiped God with sacrifices. The sacrifices God especially wants from us are our praise and thanks to him each day. Let us continually offer up a sacrifice of praise to God, just as the Lord Jesus practiced quiet times during his earthly ministry. Often, after a full day and evening, he still got up early to pray (Mark 1:35). We can do no better than to follow his example.

In your quiet time, you may want to keep a small notebook with a log of the passages you have studied and notes, observations, and applications drawn from those passages. You may also find it helpful to keep a record of your prayer requests in this notebook. Write down the special request you are praying for, then the date you began praying it, and finally, the date when your prayer is answered. After you have finished praying, you may want to just be quiet before the Lord for a few minutes. It is often at that time that he will bring some Scripture or biblical concept to your mind that you can meditate on.

Remember the importance of having a daily quiet time. Don't stand the Lord up by getting too busy to stop for a few minutes to meet with him for communication and worship and praise. Love him and tell him you enjoy His presence. He seeks your worship.

Scriptures for Study

1. *Acts 17:10.* Identify several practices of the people from the city of Berea that identified them as noble-minded.
2. *Ezra 7:10.* What three things became part of Ezra's lifestyle?
3. *Hebrews 13:15.* What forms of worship can we offer to God in a daily quiet time?
4. *Psalm 119:11.* What was the method the psalmist would use to keep his life on the right track each day?
5. *Psalm 119:92–93.* What was the key to the psalmist's experience of overcoming his problems?
6. *Psalm 119:165.* What was an inner result in the psalmist's emotions as a result of his commitment to the Word?

Additional Study

It was previously observed that Jesus frequently arose early in the morning to spend time with God. Search through the Scriptures to find out what other individuals invested time in their relationship with God early in the morning. What other activities of spiritual significance began or were carried out early in the day? (You may need a concordance to find this information. Start by looking up such words as "early" or "morning" as they occur in the New Testament.)

Scripture Passage	Activity	Applications for Me

Family Devotions

7

Memorize: Deuteronomy 6:6–7, Ephesians 6:1–4

If you have a family, have you discovered how wonderful it is for your family to have a worship time together each day? Some families have ten or fifteen minutes set aside each day for Bible reading and prayer that involves all the members in fellowship. Some combine the family devotion time with the individuals' quiet time; others keep the family and personal times separated.

Do you know that having family devotions makes for healthier marriages and home life? Statistics indicate that in many of our major cities in the United States, one out of every two marriages ends in divorce. Though only one out of forty marriages of those who regularly attend church ends in divorce, only one out of four hundred marriages end in divorce when the family reads the Bible and prays together.

Joshua said, ". . . as for me and my household, we will serve the LORD" (Josh. 24:15). God said about Abraham, "For I have chosen him, so that he will direct his children and his household after him to keep the way of the LORD . . ." (Gen. 18:19). The Philippian jailer was told by Paul and Silas: "Believe in the Lord Jesus, and you will be saved—you and your household" (Acts 16:31).

Spiritually mature leaders for the church were to be men whose children believed (Titus 1:6), who as fathers were good managers of their children (1 Tim. 3:12), and who brought them up in the discipline and instruction of the Lord (Eph. 6:4). The Israelites were told to teach God's commandments diligently to their children: ". . .Talk about them when you sit at home and when you walk along the road, when you lie down and when you get up" (Deut. 6:7).

The family of one of us chooses the breakfast table as the place and time when the family will be together each day. The father reads the Bible out loud for the family to hear, generally no more than twenty verses. Another family takes a specific time during the evening meal or immediately after it is concluded.

An idea you might try in your own home is having everyone pick out one verse or phrase that seems important to him or her for that day. It might be a happy verse of encouragement, a project that can be lived that day, or a special step of growth in lifestyle or in exercising faith. The others listen as each in turn briefly comments on why he or she has chosen that particular message from heaven for that day.

Family members might take turns praying, with a different person praying each day for the other family members, and their needs, for thanksgiving, for guidance, and so on. You could keep track of whose turn it is by using a 3 × 5 card as a book marker. For variety you might want to read from different translations of the Bible throughout the course of a year. This keeps the process fresh and stimulating.

Some families like to keep devotions to no more than fifteen minutes at the most. When children are involved, it is important to keep any scheduled program short and interesting. With young children it might be better to read aloud short Bible stories that relate to a specific Bible passage. Some books we have used or recommended include *Devotions for the Children's Hour* and *Stories for the Children's Hour* by Kenneth Taylor. There are also many other good Bible storybooks in libraries and Christian bookstores.

You might like to try one of the following methods or projects:

1. Read through the entire Bible in one year. We don't recommend that this be done as part of the family devotions but in your private quiet time, since it requires considerable reading. You would have to read three chapters from the Old Testament and one from the New Testament each day. This is an excellent preparation for family devotions.

2. The SPECS method is an interesting way to have family devotions. After each person is assigned one of the letters of this acrostic, all members look for their particular item as the head of the family reads through a passage from the Bible. Then, after the passage is read, each person talks about the project item he or she has found:

S ins to Confess—any sins mentioned in the passage that we should be willing to confess to God if we have committed them.

P romises to Claim—usually there is one special promise that will stand out (if there is more than one).

E xamples to Follow—ones we can live today from what is seen in the passage.

C ommands to Obey—pick out one special command to be obeyed today.

S tumbling Blocks—what to avoid as we relate to other people today.

3. Pick out one book of the Bible to read through little by little at each family devotion time until it is completed. We like to underline key verses, often writing them down to carry with us and look at later through the day or to memorize.

4. Memorizing key verses, perhaps one a week, would be a nice project for each member of the family.

What do you think about this aspect of your Christian life? How much is your family worth to you? At first everyone may not want to participate, especially if some are adults or older teens. If that is the case, start out with those who want to be a part. The enthusiasm will spread. Watch out for the devil, though; he will try to break up your pattern. Be determined!

Scriptures for Study

1. *Deuteronomy 6:7.* What are the *two* verbs in this verse that describe action parents can take with the Word of God in relationship to their children?

2. *Psalm 78:1–4.* In verse four, identify *three* things the psalmist lists as goals for showing the Word to the generation to come.

3. *Ezra 8:21.* Ezra and his people were interested in God's guidance for what *three* interests they had?

4. *Ephesians 6:4.* Who especially is identified as the person responsible for the spiritual training of the children?

5. *2 Timothy 3:15.* When had Timothy first learned the facts about the importance of personal faith in Christ Jesus?

Personal Projects

1. Give careful attention to Deuteronomy 6 and 2 Timothy 3. In examining 2 Timothy 3:15–17, isolate five important factors that can ultimately be covered in family devotions. Prepare a chart that identifies the item and other passages that reinforce this concept.

List the concept's application to your family's life. (The example of "salvation" will get you started.)

Factors	Related Passages	Application
Salvation	Acts 16 (Philippian Jailer) Luke 19 (Zacchaeus)	Make sure each family member has trusted Christ or at least understands what salvation involves.

Using the chart as a guide, encourage each member of the family to look for opportunities to share Christ with others as a result of any material studied in family devotions.

2. Brainstorm on ways to make your family Bible study more creative and meaningful for every member. Include such things as role playing, videos of Bible stories, and so on. Implement these. Look for opportunities to put them into practice, then list the results.

Idea	Date Tried	Result or Response

Scripture Meditation and Memorization

8

Memorize: Psalm 119:11; Colossians 3:16

Meditating on Scripture is more than just reading the Bible. The word *meditation* means to ponder, to imagine, to converse with oneself, to muse. Meditating on God's Word helps it to enter our subconscious mind much faster and thus become part of our thinking and way of life.

There are many special promises of God's blessings for an individual who meditates on God's Word. Some examples are: "But his delight is in the law of the LORD, and on his law he meditates day and night. . . . Whatever he does prospers" (Ps. 1:2–3), and ". . . meditate on it day and night, so that you may be careful to do everything written in it. Then you will be prosperous and successful" (Josh. 1:8).

In a controlled study among seminary students, we discovered that there was a marked difference between those with exceptionally sound mental health and maturity and others with "normal" or below-average mental health and maturity. These results were derived from research that included psychological testing and an extensive spiritual-life questionnaire. The difference was marked by the practice of meditation on the Word by the first group over a period of three years or longer.

One of the approaches we like for meditation has these three basic steps: (1) memorize a key verse; (2) personalize the verse by putting your name in the place of appropriate pronouns; and (3) visualize yourself acting out the verse in a probable life situation. This can be done for ten minutes or so in the morning and likewise sometime each evening.

This process can help you become successful in breaking sinful habits, overcoming besetting sins, preparing for effective witnessing, and desensitizing anxiety over meeting or confronting someone or giving a speech before a large audience. The promise is that you will have success as you do God's will.

In his book *Meditating for Success,* Paul Meier recommends this plan:

1. Go to a quiet place. Occasionally vary the place by going out alone to a lake or stream.
2. Find a comfortable position (but preferably not lying prone).
3. Relax your whole mind and body, including the various muscle groups.
4. Pray that the Holy Spirit will guide you into applicable truths as you read God's Word.
5. Read consecutively through the Bible, but don't place any legalistic guidelines on yourself (e.g., "four chapters a day").
6. When you come to a verse that jumps out at you, offers you real comfort, or otherwise confronts you with a needed behavioral change, stop and meditate for several minutes on that verse or even one phrase within the verse.
7. As you meditate on that single principle from Scripture, think of ways to appropriate personally that principle into your everyday behavior. Passively resist other unrelated thoughts and worries that intrude on your mind.

Results we can expect from meditating on the Word can include greater knowledge of the Bible and thus understanding of who God is, greater personal application of scriptural principles, lower blood pressure and other beneficial physiological responses, a longer life of usefulness here on earth for the Lord, an increasing ability to deal with anxieties, greater awareness of personal blindspots, and greater success in family life and business.

Scriptures for Study

1. *Psalm 1:2.* What attitude does the psalmist have that helps him practice meditation on the Word as he does?
2. *Psalm 1:3.* In what *two* ways is the spiritual life of the person who meditates on the Word like a tree that is well watered?
3. *Joshua 1:8.* Identify the results that would come to Joshua's life if he meditated and acted on the Word.
4. *Psalm 119:78.* Meditation on the Word helped the psalmist cope with what kind of adverse situation?
5. *Psalm 119:97.* Since it is impractical for most people to be reading the Bible throughout the course of the day, the psalmist found another way to enjoy the Word. What was his method?

6. *Psalm 119:11.* What phrase suggests memorizing the Word of God in this verse and what benefits are indicated?

Personal Project

Begin memorizing Psalm 1. Work on one verse each day for six days. Say the verse to yourself, phrase by phrase and over and over, until you have it committed to memory. Write out the verse on a 3 × 5 card. Review the verse in your mind. Then implement the steps for meditation listed in the preceding material and fill in the following chart.

Monday—*Psalm 1:1*

Memorized _____ Reviewed _____

Times I thought about the verse each day _______________

____

Circumstances under which I thought about the verse _____

____

____

Ways I began applying the verse: _______________________

____

____

Tuesday—*Psalm 1:2*

Memorized _____ Reviewed _____

Times I thought about the verse each day _______________

____

Circumstances under which I thought about the verse _____

____

____

Ways I began applying the verse ______________________________

____

____

Wednesday—*Psalm 1:3*

Memorized ______ Reviewed ______

Times I thought about the verse each day ____________________

____

Circumstances under which I thought about the verse ______

____

____

Ways I began applying the verse ______________________________

____

____

Thursday—*Psalm 1:4*

Memorized ______ Reviewed ______

Times I thought about the verse each day ____________________

____

Circumstances under which I thought about the verse ______

____

____

Ways I began applying the verse ______________________________

____

____

Friday—*Psalm 1:5*

Memorized ______ Reviewed ______

Times I thought about the verse each day ____________________

____

Circumstances under which I thought about the verse ______

____

____

Ways I began applying the verse ______________________

____

____

Saturday—*Psalm 1:6*

Memorized ______ Reviewed ______

Times I thought about the verse each day ______________

____

Circumstances under which I thought about the verse ______

____

____

Ways I began applying the verse ______________________

____

____

The Triune God

9

Memorize: Matthew 28:19; John 14:16–17

There are many things about our great God that are beyond our intellectual capacity to understand. Yet God has chosen to reveal himself to us in ways we can grasp, so that we are enabled to know him personally and to enter into a personal relationship with him. Let us review several things we know about him:

God is the cause behind the effects of our universe.

God is the Designer behind the master plan we see in nature and the universe, the Creator of the world and of man.

God is spirit, as opposed to a physical body (except as in Christ, now our risen and ascended Lord).

God is personal as opposed to a thing or a great power, for example.

God is self-existent, as opposed to us, who are dependent upon him and others for existence.

God is eternal, having had neither a beginning nor an ending.

God never changes in his character.

God knows all there is to know about everything all at once.

God is everywhere present at all times.

God can do anything he wills to do; nothing is impossible to him.

God is characterized as holy, faithful, loving, merciful, and full of grace and truth.

One of God's mysteries is that he is a Triune God. This means that although there is only one God, in the unity of the Godhead there are three eternal and co-equal persons. They are one in essence and co-equal in all things. These three persons are the Father, the Son, and the Holy Spirit. Our small and finite minds cannot intellectually understand this truth, which is infinite and far beyond what has been revealed to us. We wonder how one God can be revealed in three distinct persons. Are there three Gods? No. Is Jesus God? Yes. Is the Holy Spirit God? Yes. Is the Father God? Yes. Are there three Gods? No, only one.

Here is where the human mind must admit its limitations, where we must say, "I can't understand it, but I believe it because the Bible says that is the way it is." God does not reveal himself at one time with the mask of the Father and then at another time take off that mask and put on the mask of the Son, and at yet another time put on the mask of the Holy Spirit. That's not the way it is!

Several times in Scripture, the three persons are on the scene at the same time and yet identified as distinct from the other. One such incident is at the baptism of the Lord Jesus. While the Lord Jesus was in the water being baptized by John, the Holy Spirit came down to him in the form of a dove, and the voice of approval came from the Father in heaven. The Triune God was involved in creation when God said, "Let us make man in *our* image." The trinity is implied in other places, both in the Old Testament and the New, which will be part of your exercise in this lesson.

Illustrations of the Trinity always fall short. For example, an egg is one, yet it has three parts—but each part is only one-third of the egg. The Lord Jesus is not one third of the one God. He is God, and the Father is God, and the Holy Spirit is God, yet there is only one God. Water can be revealed in three ways—as a solid (ice), a liquid, and a gas (steam)—yet it is water. Again the illustration fails. The fact is that no human mind can sufficiently explain this mystery of our God.

Though we are not always in the understanding business, we are always in the believing business. When we pray, we should worship our God for who he is and thank him for revealing enough about himself so we could know him in a saving relationship that benefits our lives on a daily basis.

Scriptures for Study

1. *John 4:24.* What does this verse teach that contradicts the concept of God as a physical person?

2. *John 3:16.* What does this verse say God can do as a person that a great power or thing cannot do?

3. *Genesis 1:26–27.* How does this passage suggest the Trinity and yet also that God is one God?

4. *Isaiah 48:12, 16.* In these two Old Testament verses, how do you see the Trinity suggested?

5. *John 1:1.* In this verse Jesus is referred to as the Word. He is also identified in what other way?

6. *John 14:8–9.* What was the most important way in which God made himself knowable to his creatures?

7. *Matthew 28:19.* In this verse, containing the Great Commission, the baptismal formula is to be "in the name" (singular) of the Trinity. Do you see the idea of one God in the persons cited in this formula?

Personal Project

For many Christians the doctrine of the Trinity is a theoretical and abstract concept with little practical significance. Yet, if we relate each member of the Trinity to us, we can see great practical significance. As human beings created by God, we have a need for a sense of belonging, of worth, and of competence. Use the following outline to develop how each member of the Trinity individually contributes to your personal significance:

John 1:12

Person in the Trinity ______________________________

Belonging/worth/competence ______________________________

Personal insights and applications ______________________________

____

____

2 Corinthians 5:18

Person in the Trinity ______________________________

Belonging/worth/competence ______________________________

Personal insights and applications ______________________________

____

____

Romans 5:15

Person in the Trinity ______________________

Belonging/worth/competence ______________________

Personal insights and applications ______________________

____

____

Ephesians 1:3–6

Person in the Trinity ______________________

Belonging/worth/competence ______________________

Personal insights and applications ______________________

____

____

1 John 3:1–3

Person in the Trinity ______________________

Belonging/worth/competence ______________________

Personal insights and applications ______________________

____

____

John 14:15–26

Person in the Trinity ______________________

Belonging/worth/competence ______________________

Personal insights and applications ______________________

____

____

Selecting a Local Church 10

Memorize: Hebrews 10:25; 1 John 1:7

God's primary plan for carrying out his work in the world today is through his church. The church is not a building or a particular denomination, but the family of God, which is made up of individuals like you and me all across the world who have trusted Christ as Savior.

The church is called the body of Christ because it is Christ's way of expressing his love and communicating to the world in bodily form. The only physical hands that the head of the church, the Lord Jesus, has in the world today to do his work are your hands and mine. The only physical lips that he has in the world to witness and encourage others are your lips and mine, as we yield ourselves to him each day.

The church universal is manifested in local assemblies, or "churches." A local church is a group of believers that meets together regularly to worship God, to study the Word of God, to support one another in prayer, love, encouragement, accountability, growth, and to work as a team to help spread the good news of Christ to others locally and around the world.

A local church offers opportunities for individual believers to exercise their spiritual gifts in building up the members of the whole body of Christ. It also provides for financial aid to those who serve the body, to missionaries, and to those with special needs. A church is like an extended family. Its officers are pastors, also called elders (with usually one senior pastor), and deacons, who are special helpers to the church in practical ways. We would encourage you to join a good local church and be a vital and faithful participant in its work.

How do you go about selecting a local church? Here are some suggestions:

1. Don't pick a local church on the basis of the beauty of its buildings, the size of its choir, or the convenience of location.

2. Don't choose a local church merely because that is where your relatives have always gone or where your friends attend now.
3. Don't take a church for granted. Ask questions about what the church believes and practices. Ask for a church constitution and articles of faith.

Make sure the church believes in and teaches the following fundamentals of the Christian faith: the deity of Christ (that Jesus is God, the second person of the Trinity); salvation of the individual from sin by grace (without works, merit, or essential ceremonies, but through simple faith in Christ alone); the practice of baptism and communion by believers (not as a means for "making" a person into a Christian);* the verbal or word-for-word inspiration of all the Bible—resulting in a trustworthy, inerrant, and complete written revelation of God to man.

The church you select should also have a healthy balance of three programs, like the equal legs of a tripod. The first leg is sound doctrine—the teaching of the Word of God should be strong. The second leg is an emphasis on evangelism—there should be a heart for reaching people with the gospel of Christ so they can know Christ and his salvation. The third leg is a strong relational program of fellowship that encourages small-group sharing and love for one another on a more intimate level than is possible in the congregation as a whole.

This is the Church Age, and God is working through his church. Be an important part of a vital Bible-teaching local church that exalts the Lord Jesus Christ.

Scriptures for Study

1. *Ephesians 1:22–23.* The last word (usually) in verse 22 is defined in what way in the first part of verse 23?

2. *Colossians 1:18.* Who is identified as the true head of the church?

3. *Acts 2:41.* After having been saved, what first step was then taken by the new believers, according to this verse?

---

*Although the authors believe immersion in water to be the most accurate mode of baptism, there are strong, Bible-believing churches that hold to other modes of baptism. The mode, of course, has no bearing on one's eternal salvation.

4. *Acts 2:42.* What additional practices did the believers share together in the church in Jerusalem?

5. *Hebrews 10:25.* What is the Lord's will about meeting with fellow believers, and what is a purpose each of us has in this activity?

6. *Revelation 1:20.* In this verse, how does the Lord Jesus describe the function of faithful churches in this dark world?

Personal Project

Pretend you as an individual or your family has moved to a specific area. Using the material in this chapter and carefully examining Acts 2:41–42, develop a list of key areas to examine regarding potential local churches. Under each area of consideration develop a list of questions to be asked. Start with "evangelism," using sample questions in this area as a primer for four other areas of concern.

11 Building a Christian Support System

Memorize: Hebrews 13:16; James 5:16

God promises to meet our real needs as his children. He does this directly and indirectly by working through the lives of yielded believers, people he brings into our lives to minister to each of us in special ways. We, in turn, find fulfillment in yielding ourselves to the Holy Spirit so that he may work through our lives as his channels of blessing to fellow believers.

There are many ways we are to support one another as believers. We are encouraged to be devoted to one another and to choose to do loving acts. We are not to criticize, but are to accept, counsel, serve, and bear one another's burdens. As Christians, we are to be patient, encouraging and praying for one another. We are called to be hospitable and to clothe ourselves with humility toward fellow believers.

Sometimes we may actually need to confront another believer, speaking the truth in love. Yet, generally, steps of positive encouragement are the most common ways of supporting one another. These qualities can usually be best developed in small-group or one-on-one situations.

The place to start in building a Christian support system could begin by attending a good local church. Within the program of the church will be opportunities to join smaller groups, such as a Sunday-school class.

But a strong support system needs something beyond a Sunday-school class. Some churches offer small-group Bible studies that meet in homes or other informal places. Other such groups are sometimes called mini-churches, or share groups, with perhaps eight or nine couples who share fellowship in their homes weekly, twice a month, or monthly. They study the Word together, share encouragement, enjoy social activities, pray for each other, and generally encourage spiritual growth and personal evangelism.

Another method revolves around a discipleship group. This can be a group of four persons (although a smaller or larger number can be used), usually of the same sex, who are committed to study the Word in a systematic way, applying the Word to their own lives and being personally accountable to each other. If such a program is not available through your church, ask your pastor for ideas on how you could start one.

Consider whether you have some Christian friends who would like to be part of your group. Would the pastor have some suggestions for other potential members? Could one of the group act as a leader? Does the pastor have a suggested plan of Bible study—perhaps the Navigators series or a specific book of the Bible to study or this Minirth-Meier Bible-study book?

It is also helpful to develop a close friendship with one or two other Christians of the same sex who can be supportive when you need to share your feelings, frustrations, and burdens. These very special friends would not mind a phone call from you at any time you need their word of encouragement or prayers. Having breakfast or lunch occasionally together and going fishing or golfing or shopping together can be activities to share on the lighter side.

A word of caution is needed here. It takes time to develop close friendships, so be patient. Someone once stated that the average person has only about six close friends outside of his or her own family in a lifetime.

Since that is probably true, if you are looking for Christian friendships (and we hope you are), pray for God's help. Be willing to be a friend. Look for ways to initiate fellowship and to meet needs in the lives of others. Don't just wait for others to come to you. Go after what you believe God wants you to have to strengthen your spiritual life. Starting through your local church, if possible, work at building a Christian support system for yourself.

Scriptures for Study

1. *Hebrews 13:15–16.* Besides worshiping God with praise and thanksgiving, what other purpose does God have for our lives?

2. *Hebrews 10:24.* How does this verse suggest ways we gain and give support to one another?

3. *James 5:16.* How were the emotional and spiritual wounds of some believers to be healed?

4. *1 Thessalonians 2:7–8.* List some of the words and phrases in these verses that describe the way the apostle Paul was supportive of his friends.

5. *Romans 16:5.* What clue about the size of some of the churches in Bible times gives you an idea of how a more personal support to one another was given?

6. *Titus 2:1–10.* If you are an older Christian, what ministry ideas do you gain from these verses in connection with young people who are open to your help?

Additional Study

1. Develop a study on friendship based on the following passages: Proverbs 17:17, Proverbs 18:24, and Proverbs 27. Examine these passages and then complete the following outline.

Proverbs 17:17

Prerequisites for friendship ______________________

____

____

Characteristics of a good friend ______________________

____

____

Benefits provided by friendship ______________________

____

____

Proverbs 18:24

Prerequisites for friendship ______________________

____

____

Characteristics of a good friend ______________________

____

____

Benefits provided by friendship ______________________

____

____

Proverbs 27

Prerequisites for friendship ________________________

____

____

Characteristics of a good friend ____________________

____

____

Benefits provided by friendship ______________________

____

____

2. Examine the relationship between David and Jonathan (1 Sam. 18–20). List the things Jonathan did for David, things David and Jonathan had in common, and the significance of the things Jonathan did for David. Consider how they showed their friendship and the significance of that for us today.

Sharing Your Faith

12

Memorize: Romans 1:16; 1 Peter 3:15

Would you not feel an awesome sense of responsibility if you were asked to deliver some free medication to someone who would soon die without it? And what tremendous joy you would experience if the sick person recovered because of your part in delivering the cure to him!

While the above is just an analogy, the real and awesome fact is that people are lost without Christ as their Savior. Most of them are not exactly aware of their condition and even if they were, most do not know what to do to be saved. The risen Christ has given us the opportunity to be partners with him by passing on to others the "cure" to their sin problem, the good news of Christ's death for our sins. His resurrection seals the offer of eternal life as a free gift to be received by faith in Christ as our personal Savior.

How do you go about the task of sharing your faith? First, your own life needs to be clean before God. You should be yielded to the Holy Spirit and fully controlled by him. His powers give us the love we need for God and for others and the freedom and boldness we need in sharing.

Second, the unsaved often need to see the lifestyle of a Christian who has become their friend before they are ready and willing to hear the message about Christ and how to be saved. A lifestyle that demonstrates God's love by caring for people's needs, that shows confidence in God's promises for guidance and hope during the issues and trials of life, is often what the Holy Spirit uses to develop a spiritual hunger in the hearts of the unsaved.

A probing question we like to use when the Lord has opened an opportunity to witness is: "Has anyone ever taken the time to show you from the Bible how you can know you are going to heaven when you die?" If the person says no and appears interested, he or she can be shown four basic truths by using a simple visual-aid tool. Sometimes we write out the word SPAT in an acrostic form, arranging the letters from top to bottom and writing out four key words from each of the four letters. (This word has no special meaning for us, but it is merely a convenient help for remembering.)

S inner	Each one of us in the human race is a sinner. We use Romans 3:23 and explain that "all" includes ourselves as well as the friend with whom we are sharing these facts.
P enalty	We show the person Romans 6:23, especially the first part, explaining that while God loves us, he is also holy and must punish sin. If we received our "wages" from God for our sin, we would not go to heaven, but would experience death—eternal separation from God.
A tonement	Romans 5:8 explains how God's love for us moved him to give his Son to become our sacrifice and pay for our sins on the cross. Christ became our substitute and took our judgment so we would be forgiven. He arose the third day and now we have a choice (which leads into the "T").
T rust	Romans 10:13 is a good verse to explain how to trust Christ. This is like turning your case over to a doctor. It involves committing to the Lord Jesus Christ your need to be forgiven and accepted by God. You can offer to help others express their trust in a prayer, which they will repeat phrase by phrase if they really mean it. It is often both a tearful and a joyful time when a friend trusts Christ and invites him into his or her life. Another person has been saved, become a child of God, and started on a new adventure of life with the Lord in his or her heart and a future home in heaven waiting.

Another acrostic that can be used in similar fashion is SPPT. Sins/Penalty/Paid/Trust.

Who will care for your dearest friends and family members if you will not? Let the Lord burden your heart to pray for them. It is important to be patient, since sometimes there is slow progress in their becoming open to the good news. If some are not interested, we can only pray and be ready to witness. Since only God can convict individuals of their need to trust Christ, their rejection of Christ is not a rejection of us.

Mark the verses suggested above in the inside cover of your Bible. Memorize them so you can share your faith even when a Bible is not handy. Then ask the Lord to make you his channel for sharing your faith with someone.

Scriptures for Study

1. *Mark 16:15.* What are the "marching orders" the risen Lord Jesus Christ gave to his disciples and to us?
2. *John 20:21.* What special blessing is promised to those who respond to Christ's commission?
3. *Acts 1:8.* What was an important purpose for the power of the indwelling Holy Spirit?
4. *Titus 2:3–10.* Can you pick out at least *three* phrases that connect a believer's lifestyle to the effect the Word of God will have on people?
5. *Romans 10:1.* In this verse, which example from the life of the apostle Paul shows a good practice on which we can base our witnessing?

Personal Projects

1. A witness can be defined as one who gives firsthand evidence or information about what he has experienced. Jesus illustrated several principles for being a witness to him in his contact with the woman at the well. Read John 4:1–26 and complete the following outline, using verse 4 as an example.

Verse	Action Jesus Took	Significance for Us
4	He went through an area where there were unsaved people.	We should develop opportunities in our lives for friendly contact with unsaved people.
7		
10		
13–14		
17–18		
21–24		
26		

2. *Colossians 4:2–4.* Successful Christian witnessing can be affected to a great degree by our prayer lives. Look at these verses that give us instruction on how we should pray and identify *three* of them.

What *three* things should we pray for (vv. 3–4)?

Resisting Temptation

13

Memorize: 1 Corinthians 10:13; Hebrews 4:15–16

Temptations are the common experiences of each one of us as believers. Some Christians are greatly troubled because they mistakenly think that once they are saved they can no longer be tempted to do wrong. Then, when they are tempted, they feel guilty. The fact is that being tempted is not a sin, but *yielding* to temptation is. The Lord Jesus Christ was tempted directly by the devil and experienced every type of temptation that we do. There is no temptation you face that our risen Lord does not understand and empathize with you.

Our temptations to sin never come from God but originate from three sources: the world, the flesh, and the devil.

"The world" refers to our culture's system of values, philosophies, and lifestyles that leave God out. We are often tempted to tune out God when Sunday is over and we begin the new week in the workplace or at school. Our ethics and language can be so easily conformed to the world's standards.

"The flesh" refers to our sin nature, which we all have within us, even as believers. This refers to our capacity to think evil thoughts and to sin.

Then there is "the devil." His war is with God, but one of his tactics is to divert us from God's will to his way in an attempt to deprive God of the honor and obedience he deserves from us. Satan will always tempt us by appealing to certain needs in our lives. He offers to fulfill them, but by violating God's Word in the process and thus insulting God. The devil tempts us away from God, away from Bible reading, away from prayer, away from Christian friends and church. Each one of us has a particular weakness, and Satan will try to learn what it is and how to make his temptations strong and hard to resist in that area.

The good news is that we can resist temptations and thus triumph in Christ. The first thing to understand is that God always supervises the load limits on us at any one time. When driving on country roads you may frequently see bridges with signs reading "Load Limit 10 Tons" or something similar. In the same fashion, our temptation limit is supervised by God. If you will think about it, you can probably recall a number of times when God intervened in your life just in time. He will not allow us to be tempted beyond our capacity if we draw upon the resources he has made available to us. Consider some of these sources:

1. *Our legal freedom from bondage to our old master, Satan.* A slave in the Roman Empire would remain a slave until death, either the death of his master or his own death. The apostle Paul says that each believer in Christ has died in a certain sense. We died with Christ on the cross. The old person we were before salvation was crucified with Christ. We are alive now, with Christ's resurrected life within us. We can say no to Satan's bluff if we choose to do so. We are free from his dominion. We have found it helpful at times to confess this affirmation out loud by saying: "I am dead to sin and Satan, but alive unto God."

2. *The sword of the Spirit, which is the Word of God.* Memorize verses of Scripture that relate to the areas in which you are most often tempted. Quote the Scripture to yourself when you feel the pressures of temptation. Use this as your weapon. Remember, when Jesus was tempted by Satan, at each point of temptation he stated, "It is written" (Matt. 4:1–11).

3. *The intercessory prayers of our Great High Priest in heaven.* The Lord Jesus Christ is our intercessor, and this is an important part of God's plan for our victory.

4. *Courage* to run away from sources of temptation.

5. *The power of prayer* is effective.

6. *The encouragement of godly friends,* even perhaps someone with whom you could establish an accountability.

7. *The indwelling Holy Spirit* releases his power from within, and "the one who is in you is greater than the one who is in the world" (1 John 4:4).

We do have temptations, but experiencing temptation is not a sin. James 1:15 explains that lust must "conceive" to bring forth sin. What this means is that only when temptation is yielded to does sin occur.

Let us prepare for the battles ahead of time by reviewing our resources, memorizing key Scriptures, and committing ourselves to walk with our Lord, enjoying ever-increasing intimacy with him.

Scriptures for Study

1. *1 Corinthians 10:13.* List *three* facts we should learn about temptations from this verse.

2. *Hebrews 4:15.* How does this verse assure us that our Savior understands our pressures and sympathizes with us?

3. *James 1:13–14.* According to these verses, where does temptation to sin never come from? What is it within each of us that entices us to respond to temptation?

4. *Romans 6:6, 11.* When did we die, in a legal sense? Since death death become a practical and freedom-maintaining experience in daily life?

5. *Luke 22:31–32.* What resource do we have in our favor to help us use faith against temptations, as seen in these verses?

6. *Matthew 26:41.* What responsibilities are suggested in this verse for resisting temptations?

Additional Study

According to Galatians 5:23, one fruit of the Spirit is "self-control." The basic idea behind this word is that the inner strength provided by the Holy Spirit will help you say no to temptation.

For the following verses list what the verse tells you to think, what the verse tells you to do, and what personal application you can identify.

Romans 6:13

Think ____

____

____

Do ____

____

____

Application ____

____

____

Proverbs 4:25

Think ______________________________

____

____

Do ______________________________

____

____

Application ______________________________

____

____

Job 31:1

Think ______________________________

____

____

Do ______________________________

____

____

Application ______________________________

____

____

Matthew 4:1–11

Think ______________________________

____

____

Do ______________________________

____

____

Application ______________________________________

____

____

Psalm 119:9

Think ______________________________________

____

____

Do ______________________________________

____

____

Application ______________________________________

____

____

Psalm 119:11

Think ______________________________________

____

____

Do ______________________________________

____

____

Application ______________________________________

____

____

Hebrews 11:24–25

Think ______________________________________

____

____

Do ______________________________________

____

____

Application ________________________________

____

____

Personal Project

Make a record of your personal struggle with temptations over a set period of time. Make a chart and list the following:

1. The temptation(s)
2. How you responded—successfully or unsuccessfully
3. Passage of Scripture you used or could have used
4. How you prepared yourself to successfully face this temptation in the future.

Our Struggle from Within

14

Memorize: Romans 6:11; Hebrews 12:1–2

One of the authors has revealed the following about one aspect of his experience as a Christian: "I remember the time I first trusted Christ as my personal Savior. I was so happy; I felt so clean. I can remember thinking to myself, 'Now that I am saved, I won't do wrong anymore.' It wasn't too long after that thought that I discovered I could still sin by thoughts, words, and deeds. I was disappointed. However, through some Bible teaching I learned that every believer still has a sin nature in him that has the capacity and instinct to be self-centered and rebellious to God."

Each of us can probably identify with those words. In fact, the apostle John describes our struggle from within as "the lust of the flesh and the lust of the eyes and the boastful pride of life" (1 John 2:16). The word *lust,* strictly speaking, means strong craving and is not necessarily undesirable or sexually oriented. For example, the Holy Spirit lusts for our devotion, as the King James Version (James 4:5) suggests. And it is proper for a married person to have a strong desire (lust) and attraction toward his or her spouse.

On the other hand, strong desires that come from an unchecked sin nature lead us to transgression. Pursuing these lusts draws away our love for God, and our investment is instead given to the world. The word *world* used in this context means society's system of values and thinking that are hostile toward God and compete for the Christian's priorities and love.

"Lust of the flesh" causes one type of personal struggle. This refers to physical and emotional appetites that go beyond God's will for our lives. In every believer there is pressure to follow the world's philosophy of life, which says, "If it feels good, do it." Yielding to this attitude can lead to extramarital affairs, drunkenness, drugs, gluttony, wild partying, laziness, disorderliness, impulsiveness, and so on.

The apostle Paul describes the lifestyle of the unsaved world of his day as catering to a desire-oriented and pleasure-motivated people: "Having lost all sensitivity, they have given themselves over to sensuality, so as to indulge in every kind of impurity, with a continual lust for more" (Eph. 4:19).

"Lust of the eyes" is another part of the struggle from within. This refers to our appetite for what others have, though that may not be God's will for us or at least in God's timing for us.

Curiosity can be a valuable human trait, but our sin nature can take control of our imagination and create covetousness and greed that becomes an obsession. In this context, our eyes are never satisfied but want to drink in more and more, which fuels the internal covetousness. God gave to Moses these instructions for the people of Israel: "You shall not covet your neighbor's house; you shall not covet your neighbor's wife . . . or anything that belongs to your neighbor" (Exod. 20:17).

The lust of the eyes can turn window-shopping into a credit extravaganza as we acquire things not needed or that cannot be afforded. It can turn sincere admiration of another person's appearance, grooming, and personal qualities into fantasies of illicit sex. It can turn a healthy pleasure in whatever God has given us to enjoy into a competitive drive to keep ahead of the Joneses. This mentality draws us away from loving God.

"Pride of life" is also part of our inner struggle. This is the drive to be important and significant for the sake of personal glory, the craving for status and praise, the desire to be able to influence and control others as a result of power plays. It is disconnected from the goal of being used by the Holy Spirit to bring honor and glory to God. This is the drive to boast of what we have and what we do.

When our lives are marked by the lust of the flesh, the lust of the eyes, or the pride of life, we are squeezed into the world's mold—something the apostle Paul warns us not to permit to happen (Rom. 12:2).

How do we deal with these pressures? God's Word says, "Do not love the world . . ." (1 John 2:15), and we have the power to make this choice each day. We can choose where we invest our affections and what we make important in our lives. There are several guidelines to keep in mind as you deal with your struggle from within.

First, *keep Christ in first place* in your life and make him your ultimate purpose for living. This includes keeping strong in the Word and using prayer on a regular basis.

Second, *turn off sin's power daily.* The apostle Paul says we render sin's power ineffective when we consider or reckon ourselves dead to the impulses and messages from our sin nature; instead we consider ourselves alive and responsive to God in Christ Jesus our Lord. A practical way this faith method works for some requires that—when tempted from without or within—you be willing to confess the affirmation "I am dead to sin and Satan, but I am alive and responsive to God." You will usually then find immediate relief from the strong impulses to sin, although this may have to be done several times in the course of the day.

Third, *walk in the Spirit,* an idea that is closely connected to step two. What is the result of walking in the Spirit? You will not fulfill the lust of the flesh. Walking in the Spirit means you conduct your daily life in dependence on the indwelling Holy Spirit.

Fourth, *meditate on Scripture.* This helps us experience Romans 12:2b: ". . . be transformed by the renewing of your mind. Then you will be able to test and approve what God's will is—his good, pleasing and perfect will." As you memorize, meditate on, and apply the Word of God, the Scripture will actually transform your thought processes, enabling you to live in a way pleasing to God.

Above all, take positive action. Do God's will. Don't remain idle, for God has many things for you to do for him. Your struggle will not go away completely, but victory can be yours on a day-to-day basis.

Scriptures for Study

1. *1 John 1:10.* Can the believer in Christ ever say in this life that he or she does not sin anymore?
2. *Romans 7:15–18.* After having been a Christian many years and a powerful missionary for Christ, what does the apostle Paul say was a primary cause of struggle within?
3. *1 John 2:15–17.* Can you identify the *three* usual forms of struggle the believer has to deal with on a day-to-day basis?
4. *Hebrews 13:5.* What is mentioned in this verse that is a character quality that counteracts coveteousness?
5. *Romans 6:11.* A responsibility each believer has in responding to the impulses of his or her sin nature is clearly given in this verse. What is it?

Additional Studies

1. The author of Hebrews gives us a view of life as a marathon race (Heb. 12:1–3). Others who are viewed as witnesses have successfully run their race. Discover and outline the lessons regarding the world that can be learned from this passage.

"Let us throw off everything that hinders"

Meaning ____

____

Significance ____

____

"Let us throw off . . . the sin that so easily entangles"

Meaning ____

____

Significance ____

____

"Let us run with perseverance"

Meaning ____

____

Significance ____

____

"Let us fix our eyes on Jesus"

Meaning ____

____

Significance ____

____

". . . the author and perfecter of our faith"

Meaning ______________________________

____

Significance ______________________________

____

"Consider him . . ." (*clue:* an engaged mind)

Meaning ______________________________

____

Significance ______________________________

____

". . . so that you will not grow weary and lose heart" (*clue:* an encouraged heart)

Meaning ______________________________

____

Significance ______________________________

____

2. What do the following verses tell us about the world and what is the significance to us?

John 12:31

About the world ______________________________

____

Significance ______________________________

____

John 7:7

About the world ______________________________

____

Significance ______________________________

____

Acts 4:27

About the world ______________________________

____

Significance ________________________________

____

John 15:19

About the world ______________________________

____

Significance ________________________________

____

Galatians 6:14

About the world ______________________________

____

Significance ________________________________

____

Colossians 3:1–3

About the world ______________________________

____

Significance ________________________________

____

1 John 2:17

About the world ______________________________

____

Significance ________________________________

____

Living by Grace

15

Memorize: Ephesians 2:8–9, Titus 3:5–6

Most of us love that old familiar song, which is still so popular today, "Amazing Grace." God's amazing grace has saved us from the penalty of our sins and through Christ has given us acceptance with God forever. That same grace will also be at work in the lives of believers on a day-to-day basis.

Let us first define "grace." It is the unmerited favor of God. Someone explained the meaning of the word by using each letter in an acrostic saying that GRACE is God's Riches At Christ's Expense. The system of grace was often contrasted by the apostle Paul to the system of law and works.

A legalistic religious system says in effect that if you do good enough, long enough, you will gain God's acceptance. Most of the world's religions are based on legalism. In fact, most people in our generation think that going to heaven is based upon doing enough good. Obviously they do not understand the gospel of grace. If God's acceptance were conditional upon our merit, we would never have any assurance or peace in this life about where we stand with God. We would also be feeding our insecurities by our religious views.

Grace, in contrast, teaches that God accepts us "up front" because of Christ whom we trusted. We have total, unconditional love and acceptance forever the moment we trust Christ as our Savior. It is an acceptance and love we did not earn but was given to us as a gift despite our faults, failures, sin, and depravity. Now, since we are "justified," or declared righteous, because of the merits of Christ given to us, God encourages us to walk with him and to grow, even though in a practical sense we fail God's Word in many ways.

As believers, our motivation is love, not fear. Our power is provided by the indwelling Holy Spirit, not by our personal will to keep the law. Our security in life has its primary basis in God's unconditional love and acceptance of us, which can never be lost.

Grace living does not require trying to compensate God for our sins by penance or other forms of "dead works." Rather, it is rooted in our belief in the position of acceptance we have in Christ as we walk with God in a loving and personal relationship every day. When we sin, we need not be fearful of losing our salvation, but of grieving the heart of our loving God. We confess our sins and accept his immediate forgiveness.

Our treatment of others should likewise be on the basis of grace, not conditional legalism. We must accept others as unconditionally as we can as human beings. Let us love people for who they are as God's creatures, not for what they do. That means trying to separate unbiblical behavior from an individual's personhood. We can assure such a person that our love for him or her as a person will continue, even though we may also express our negative feelings about behavior that we would like to see changed in that individual.

The Lord Jesus Christ was a good example of this attitude many times. For instance, a woman who was caught in the act of adultery was brought to him by people who believed she should be condemned to death. Jesus first accepted her as a person, saying, ". . . neither do I condemn you." Then he addressed her behavior by adding, "Go now and leave your life of sin" (John 8:11).

In summary, legalism is walking in fear, never knowing where you stand, but trying to earn acceptance. Grace is being totally accepted, unconditionally, then walking in love while learning and growing in one's life and relationship to God and others.

Scriptures for Study

1. *Ephesians 2:8–9.* A definition for grace is "God's unmerited favor to us because of Christ." If you substitute this definition for the word *grace,* how would these verses read? Try it.
2. *Titus 3:5.* The first part of this verse contradicts the teaching of many man-made religions. What is the plan of becoming acceptable to God as expressed by false religious teaching?
3. *John 14:21.* The Christian life involves obedience to God's Word. But what is the motivation for obedience, since we are assured of our being totally accepted by God up front?
4. *Romans 8:1–4.* Who lives in us and produces the righteous life through us as indicated in verse 4?
5. *Galatians 5:19, 22.* Verse 19 talks about works, while verse 22 describes fruit. Since fruit is a natural result of the life within a fruit tree (or a Christian), can you identify the source of the fruit of Christian graces that develop in the yielded believer's life?

Part 2

Growing Emotionally

The second part of this manual presents topics related to emotional growth, an interdependent counterpart to spiritual growth. Growing emotionally means that we begin to handle anger, fear, and bitterness as Christ would. As we seek to become more like him, one by-product will be emotional maturity—the fruit of spiritual growth. God's Holy Spirit will produce in us the fulfillment of his specific instructions on handling anger, bitterness, and worry; loving unconditionally; maintaining self-control; and experiencing joy (Gal. 5:22–23).

Particular areas of study in this section include: separating our perception of God from that of our earthly father; overcoming inferiority feelings, depression, anxiety, workaholism, burnout, failure, and suicidal tendencies; and learning to handle bitterness, anger, guilt, and grieving.

In studying how to deal biblically with our emotions, we learn to identify our emotional vulnerabilities and to apply practical ways to strengthen them. These will include Scripture meditation and memorization, sharing feelings with others who are significant in our lives, understanding our personal worth in Christ, and projects centered on these activities. This naturally enhances two basics of our spiritual growth—genuine Christian fellowship and witnessing, both of which depend heavily on our emotional maturity. Then, as we overcome emotional struggles, we can more effectively reach out to make and keep friends and to share our faith.

The Proper Perception of God

16

Memorize: 2 Corinthians 3:3–4; James 1:17

It seems obvious that there is a connection between our automatic concept of God and the perceptions we have of our natural father or whoever else was a father figure to us in our formative years. When a little child is taught his first prayers and says, "Dear heavenly Father," he is probably thinking, "Dear heavenly version of my earthly father." The word *father* identifies early in life with what we feel and believe about our earthly father. This perception of God continues, even into adulthood, unless we really dig into God's Word and get to know God intimately.

Some people think of God as a distant being, unapproachable and indifferent to their needs, because that was the way they related to their dad. Others think of God as totally negative, cold, perfectionistic, always taking note of their mistakes and wrongs but never recognizing any worth in them as a person. Again this perception develops because that may have been the way their fathers related to them. Others think of God as a big "sugar daddy," like Santa Claus, always patting them on the head, wearing thick glasses and thus never really seeing the truth—always positive, spoiling them, and never restricting or guiding them in life in any way. These people would probably say, "That's the way Daddy was to me." Still others choose to disbelieve in God completely, particularly if the father was absent from the home.

Our counseling experience indicates that the reasons for such misconceptions are usually emotional rather than intellectual. There is something painful in their past that they cope with by painting distorted pictures of God or by dismissing him from their belief entirely. That pain might even connect to some real problem with their father, but it is certainly not limited to that factor.

The truth is that God is not like *your* father or anyone else's. Your father may or may not have been a good parent. He may or may not have been loving. He may have been gone a lot, or he may have been always around when you needed him. He may have allowed you freedom to become mature, or he may have dominated your life. He may have made you "daddy's favorite child" and spoiled you by granting your every wish, or he may have seemingly neglected you. But the fact is that God—Perfect Father—is not to be compared to any earthly father, who has every human weakness in varying degrees.

Let God reveal himself to you in the ways he chooses to use. He revealed himself to us through his Son. As you trust and learn about the Lord Jesus, you can understand more about his Father. God also reveals himself through his Word, the Bible. Study the Scriptures, looking for ways God describes himself. Examine his attributes: his greatness, his grace, his love, his holiness, the meanings of his names. In fact, a good study is to identify various qualities about our heavenly Father as found in Psalm 103. See if you can be a good detective in the study that follows.

Scriptures for Study

Read Psalm 103, in which the following descriptions of God are found. Indicate which people in the listed categories seem to reflect more "godlikeness" in each of the qualities ascribed to God.

	Father	Mother	Spouse
1. Holy	☐	☐	☐
2. Righteous	☐	☐	☐
3. Just	☐	☐	☐
4. Truthful	☐	☐	☐
5. Communicative	☐	☐	☐
6. Loving	☐	☐	☐
7. Compassionate	☐	☐	☐
8. Gracious	☐	☐	☐
9. Slow to anger	☐	☐	☐
10. Patient	☐	☐	☐
11. Forgiving	☐	☐	☐
12. Understanding	☐	☐	☐
13. Rules well	☐	☐	☐

Additional Studies

1. "Attributes" are descriptions of a person's nature or character. The following Scripture passages reveal some of the Father's at-

tributes. Using the first example as a guide, identify each attribute and its significance in our lives.

John 5:26 (example)

Attribute Self-existence ____________________

Significance We are dependent on God for our existence. God depends on no one. Thus, we can trust him. ____________________

John 6:57

Attribute ____________________

Significance ____________________

____

John 10:29

Attribute ____________________

Significance ____________________

____

Romans 8:27

Attribute ____________________

Significance ____________________

____

John 14:23

Attribute ____________________

Significance ____________________

____

John 16:28

Attribute ____________________

Significance ____________________

____

Luke 10:21

Attribute ______________________________

Significance ______________________________

____

Romans 16:27

Attribute ______________________________

Significance ______________________________

____

John 17:11

Attribute ______________________________

Significance ______________________________

____

Matthew 5:48

Attribute ______________________________

Significance ______________________________

____

John 17:25

Attribute ______________________________

Significance ______________________________

____

John 3:16

Attribute ______________________________

Significance ______________________________

____

1 Corinthians 1:9

Attribute ______________________________

Significance ______________________________

____

2. Study the following passages. Identify the personal significance of God's Fatherhood. Following the first example, list what God does for us as a Father and the practical significance or application in our lives.

Matthew 6:25–33 (example)

What God does He cares for us.

Application We can trust him and not be anxious.

John 17:11; 10:29–31

What God does ______________________________

Application ______________________________

____

Matthew 7:11; James 1:17

What God does ______________________________

Application ______________________________

____

1 John 1:3, 7

What God does ______________________________

Application ______________________________

____

Matthew 5:48

What God does ______________________________

Application ______________________________

____

Hebrews 12:5–11

What God does ______________________________

Application ______________________________

____

John 16:27

What God does ______________________________

Application ______________________________

____

John 16:23

What God does ______________________________

Application ______________________________

____

Romans 8:16–17

What God does ______________________________

Application ______________________________

____

Matthew 6:32; 2 Corinthians 11:31

What God does ______________________________

Application ______________________________

____

Matthew 6:14

What God does ______________________________

Application ____

____

2 Corinthians 1:3–4

What God does ____

Application ____

____

Overcoming Failure

17

Memorize: Philippians 3:16; Proverbs 24:16

Failure is not always bad. Many times we are introduced to the road to success at the very point of failure. For example, consider the pole-vaulter. He can never reach his potential height of vaulting unless he is willing to risk failure. He experiences failure by sometimes kicking off the bar. But he "fails" in order to succeed in the long run. He measures his potential for each day at the point where he can do no better.

Let us think about some definitions. What is "success"? If it is the opposite of failure, then how can we have the right perspective about failure if we do not first have a clear definition of success?

Success is achieving the maximum of your potential in the situation you are in.[1] Success is not determined realistically by measuring yourself by someone else's achievements, appearance, wealth, whatever. You have succeeded when you can say you did the best you could do at the time. Perhaps you ask, "What else could I have done?" It is easy to be an armchair quarterback and to look at the slow-motion replay and say you could have said this differently or done that in another way. However, reality is looking back and saying you gave it your best shot. That deserves a reward—your own congratulations.

Did you know that God is pleased with you when you operate your life on the basis of the light he has given you? The apostle Paul said: "Only let us live up to what we have already attained" (Phil. 3:16). In other words, wherever you are in your Christian growth, give it your best shot. Personal success for any of us comes at the point where we cannot do any better than we are doing at this moment.

How then shall we define "failure"? *Failure is failing to give your project all that you've got.*[2] You do not fail because you make mis-

---

1. Robert H. Schuller, *Tough-Minded Faith for Tender-Hearted People* (New York: Bantam Books, 1983).
2. Ibid.

takes or do not do something perfectly, or even because you do not do something as well as you might do it sometime in the future. Failure is not doing the best you can at the moment after considering the project's relative importance and measuring that against the time and strength available for all your projects at hand.

Many times, however, we do fail to put out our best available performance. We all have self-centered tendencies and feel lazy or unmotivated at times. Failure is then compounded when we just quit. Failure is not just failing, but not trying again. We often overgeneralize and say, "If I fail at this project, I will fail at anything." Sometimes we personalize this by saying, "If I fail, that makes me a loser and a worthless person." We sometimes focus too much on a goal without taking delight in the steps of progress toward the goal.

Failure will have a hard time coming into your life if you evaluate your daily activities on the basis of doing good, consistent work rather than on measuring how far you have yet to go in order to reach some concrete or idealistic goal.

Scriptures for Study

1. *Proverbs 24:16.* What is it about a righteous and successful man that makes him different from the person who fails, since both experience falling into occasional defeat?
2. *Philippians 3:16.* Does God expect us to conduct our daily lives by standards beyond our capacity to fulfill? What is the standard for each of us, according to this verse?
3. *Mark 14:3–9.* What phrase in verse 8 indicates the Lord's confirmation of success in this action by the woman?
4. *2 Corinthians 4:8–18.* In these difficult experiences and setbacks in life, Paul was not a failure. Can you find a statement he makes at the beginning of one of the last few verses that indicates the ingredient he had in all of this that meant success?
5. *Hebrews 11:6.* What special quality in our lives pleases God, even when we face setbacks?

Additional Study

One of the most dramatic "failures" recorded in the Bible occurred when Peter denied the Lord.

1. Note the events leading up to his failure. Read the verse listed, then add what Peter did to exhibit failure and the significance to us. Use Mark 14:29 as an example.

Mark 14:29 (example)

Action Expressed overconfidence even when warned of danger of future failure.

Significance We may feel overconfident, especially if we have been successful at times in the past.

Mark 14:37

Action ______________________________

____

Significance ______________________________

____

Mark 14:54

Action ______________________________

____

Significance ______________________________

____

Mark 14:68, 70

Action ______________________________

____

Significance ______________________________

____

Mark 14:71

Action ______________________________

____

Significance ____

____

2. Was Peter's failure permanent? Examine the following verses to discover how God enabled Peter to turn failure into success. Jot down what you have learned.

Mark 14:72

John 21:4–22 (esp. 15–17)

Acts 2:14–41

Acts 4:5–13

Personal Project

Drawing upon your own life history, list on a separate piece of paper the following:

1. Personal experiences you consider to be failures
2. Steps you have taken to reverse the situation
3. Steps you can take in the future to avoid a recurrence of the situation

The Dangers of Unforgiving Bitterness

18

Memorize: Matthew 6:14–15; Ephesians 4:31–32

Sometimes people say angrily, "He doesn't deserve my forgiveness. What he has done just isn't forgivable. In fact, he's just a jerk." It may be true that this person does not "deserve" your forgiveness, but the real question is whether *you* desire mental and physical health. Do you want peace of mind? Or do you want the natural consequences of holding a grudge and perpetuating your bitterness?

Let us start by looking at anger itself. Anger is an emotional reaction involving energy. Anger is not bad in itself, because it can become very constructive. The Bible says, "In your anger [it's okay to be angry] do not sin. . ." (Eph. 4:26). That tells us that it is what we do with our anger that can make it bad.

You usually feel righteous anger when *your God-given personal rights are threatened or violated.* An example would be if your right to be regarded as the exclusive mate in a relationship were to be violated by the unfaithfulness of your marriage partner. (So-called rights that are not God-given are discussed in chapter 19.)

Another time of righteous anger is when *your personal convictions are being violated or threatened.* The Lord Jesus was angry several times, as is recorded in the Bible. He healed a man on the Jewish Sabbath, for which the Pharisees criticized him, because they thought he was breaking an important rule about not working on the Sabbath. Jesus looked around at them with anger as he stated his conviction: "The Sabbath was made for man, not man for the Sabbath" (read Mark 2:27–3:6).

When were *you* angry last? Was a personal right or conviction being violated or threatened? What did you do with your anger from that point on? You can sin with your anger when you do either of two extremes—blow up or clam up.

To "blow up" is to mix good anger with a vengeance motive. That results in a new ingredient called hostility, which is a way of getting even by physical abuse or by acting out (such as slamming doors or driving the car in a reckless manner), thus showing our indignation. We also show our anger by our words, using put-downs, name-calling, yelling, temper tantrums, threats, sarcasm, and even a hostile "silent treatment." We take the whip in our hand, so to speak, and pay back the offender. We want him to hurt as much as (or more than) he hurt us.

The other extreme is to "clam up." This style involves saying nothing about our angry feelings and holding on to a grudge. Then our anger becomes bitterness. It affects our health. It can turn into depression and even lead to suicidal thoughts. All this grieves the Lord, since it blocks our fellowship with him. The motive for holding a grudge is the same as for open hostility—vengeance. We are saying, "I will not be kind to that person until I see that somehow he has been made to suffer. I will ignore him. I will pout, or snub him." That may not even phase the other person, but it eats away at your own health, your emotional balance, and your spirit.

Be alert for the dangers of vengeance and bitterness. What is wrong with vengeance as a motive is that it is not our responsibility to be God's agents in punishing our offenders. God instructs us never to pay back evil for evil to anyone (Rom. 12:17–18). "Do not take revenge, my friends, but leave room for God's wrath [in other words, we should get out of the way so God can deal with the person], for it is written: 'It is mine to avenge; I will repay,' says the Lord" (v. 19).

You do count, and your rights are important. Somebody needs to stand up for you, but it is God who will. Turn it over to him in prayer. Don't play God by executing vengeance yourself. God instituted government, so his plan may include your turning the person over to the law. But usually human conflicts are on a more personal basis.

Anger itself is an emotion that is "neutral." It is what we do with it that determines whether it becomes a positive or negative force in our life. Valid anger can be a signal that something constructive can come out of a situation. Invalid anger—when a perceived personal right is really a selfish or perfectionistic demand—usually has negative results and therefore should not be pursued but yielded to God. (We will deal with that in the next chapter.)

Scriptures for Study

1. *Ephesians 4:26.* According to this verse, is it proper to be angry? What is the inappropriate handling of anger called?

2. *Mark 3:1–6.* Observe how the Lord Jesus experienced angry feelings. By referring back to Mark 2:27, can you see his stated conviction, which these Pharisees were violating by their rules? What was it?

3. *Leviticus 19:17–18.* What prohibitions are given at the beginning of each of these verses that should not be part of our spirit when we experience feelings of anger?

4. *Hebrews 12:15.* What *two* things are the result of bitterness?

5. *Ephesians 4:31–32.* What are we to do with our bitterness? Does verse 32 tell us how to do it? What is the way to deal with it?

6. *Matthew 18:32–35.* What could be some physical and emotional consequences that may come to the person who holds a grudge, as suggested by the word *jailers* in verse 34 (NIV)? (*Clue:* Greek word—"torturers.")

Additional Study

Look up the following references for bitterness and list the negative effects and personal application.

Colossians 3:19

Negative effects ________________________________

____

Personal application ____________________________

____

____

Hebrews 12:15

Negative effects ________________________________

____

Personal application ____________________________

____

____

James 3:10–12

Negative effects ______________________________

____

Personal application ______________________________

____

____

Ephesians 4:31–32

Negative effects ______________________________

____

Personal application ______________________________

____

____

Personal Project

Develop a personal anger chart listing several occasions when you were angry. There should be five columns, headed as follows:

1. *Circumstances* (list who or what made you feel anger)
2. *Degree of Anger* (describe whether it was minor or major and how long it lasted)
3. *Right or Conviction Violated* (describe—or write "none")
4. *Reaction* (describe what you did about your anger)
5. *Appropriateness* (your judgment about whether or not your reaction was appropriate)

Handling Anger Constructively

19

Memorize: Ephesians 4:26–27; Leviticus 19:17–18

Make sure you have read the previous chapter before reading this one because the two tie together. In chapter 18 we saw that there is a valid anger and also an anger that is invalid. Before we move on to the proper way of handling anger, let's take another look at invalid anger.

There are times when we feel angry, yet a perceived personal right that was violated was not a valid right at all. Our "right" was based on selfish demands or on perfectionistic standards. In these instances, the best thing to do is to yield such perceived rights to God. This type of anger should not be pursued with an offender since there is, in fact, no valid offender.

For example, a father is reading his newspaper when his small son jumps up into his lap and tugs at the bottom of the paper, wanting his father's attention. The father feels a surge of anger within. Why? He at first perceives that his right to read the paper without being disturbed is being violated. On second thought (if he is a good father), he realizes that this is not a valid right in light of the circumstances. It originates in a selfish or perfectionist motivation. Of course his son is more important than reading the paper, so he yields his perceived right to God, and the feeling of anger dissipates.

When feelings of anger come to you, don't express any on-the-spot words or action. Stop! Think! Is your anger valid? Then deal with it scripturally. If it is not a valid anger, let it go. Give it up to God by confessing it as a sin. Thank him for giving you the wisdom to tell the difference!

Now we will look at three things to do with anger that will lead to its proper resolution in your life.

The first thing to do is *verbalize your angry feelings.* God's Word teaches us to confront our offender if possible. Otherwise, we may be as guilty as he is. It is important to stand up for yourself and for what you believe is right, as long as you do so without feelings of vengeance or of getting even. Neither should you imply that you will seek to retaliate in the future.

To verbalize is to turn your anger feelings into words. Tell the person exactly what you feel. In doing so, you are not attacking him but confessing your own feelings. Emphasize an "I feel" message rather than a "you" accusation or a "why" question. For example, "I felt very hurt and angry when you belittled me in front of all those people."

Sometimes when the offender cannot be confronted directly, it is helpful to write out your feelings in a letter you can either send to him or might decide to just throw away. This allows you to verbalize your feelings, but in written form, which takes the potentially destructive energy out of them. David did this in some of the Psalms. He even wrote some angry words to God—look at the first part of Psalm 13. Have you ever been angry with God? Share your feelings with him. You will then be able to think more clearly about his mercy and love, which are always at work behind the scenes.

The second thing to do with anger is *commit to God all your feelings of getting even.* "'It is mine to avenge; I will repay,' says the Lord" (Rom. 12:19b). Sometimes forgiving someone, especially someone who isn't sorry, seems like you are ignoring yourself and your feelings. It makes you think, "Hey, don't I count? Should I just pretend it didn't happen?"

The thing to do is to turn over the matter to the highest power in the universe, God Himself. He has promised to deal with offenders in the way he sees as best. Leave that up to God by cleansing your mind of thoughts of revenge. Don't play God. In a prayer say, "Dear Lord, I give up any personal right to get even with so and so. I turn the matter over to you. I know you will do the right thing."

The third thing to do with your anger is *forgive the offender.* A functional description of forgiveness includes adopting the following attitude.

> By the choice of my will, not my feelings, I choose not to bring up these issues to (the offender) again. They are dead. I will not bring them up to others in the form of gossip either. Nor will I bring them up in my own meditations. I can remember what happened, but I will not brood over the past. If my thoughts begin to focus on those past

hurts, I will stop them and replace them with positive thoughts about the good things in my present life. If the person who offended me has repented, I will look for ways to eventually rebuild a friendship. If not, I will still treat him as a forgiven person, even if my feelings send me contrary messages.

I will choose to be loyal to my faith and stand by my choice to forgive. The hurts may come back from time to time for many months, but I will not act on my feelings at those moments. Instead, I will reaffirm my choice to forgive, even if I have to do it every day for a long time. My feelings will eventually catch up with my faith and my hurts will heal in time.

In summary, what should you do with your anger? Verbalize your feelings, commit the offender to God, and personally forgive. Can you do it? Will you do it now?

Scriptures for Study

Anger is the underlying cause of many emotional problems. By learning to deal with anger, we can learn to cope with other emotional struggles as well. Look up the following Scriptures and identify some constructive steps to take in resolving anger issues.

1. *Psalm 139:23–24.* In these verses, the psalmist asks God for what kind of insight?
2. *James 5:16.* How is this method of healing different from the way many people "stuff" their emotions inside themselves?
3. *Leviticus 19:17.* What does the phrase "Rebuke your neighbor [who has offended you]" mean to you as far as resolving valid anger?
4. *Ephesians 4:32.* Forgiveness here includes an attitude to develop toward the offender and a reason for forgiving, like the reason God had for forgiving us. What are these *two* keys to forgiveness?
5. *Philippians 3:13.* If forgiveness has been granted and we are still tempted to brood in self-pity over past hurt, what does this verse tell us to do?

Personal Project I

1. Can you identify your anger feelings when they exist? Answer these *two* questions: When was the last time you had a significant anger feeling? What was the situation that caused your deepest anger in the last two years?

2. Who are some people God has brought into your life with whom you can share your feelings?

3. When you have a valid anger, what are some ways for you to take a stand for what is right and for yourself so as to bring about some possible constructive results?

4. David went through many deep emotional experiences. Read the following passages to learn how he used three constructive methods—praying, singing, and writing—to verbalize his feelings. Praying: Psalm 55:12–18; singing: Psalm 57:6, 7; writing: Psalm 58 and many other Psalms.

5. In your own words, define what forgiveness means to you.

6. If forgiveness is a choice of the will, what will you do when remembered feelings of hurt come back from time to time?

Personal Project II

List individuals who have offended you and add the other information indicated.

Offender ______________________________

How he or she offended me ______________________________

____

How I responded ______________________________

____

Date I chose to forgive offender ______________________________

Action taken to rebuild relationship ______________________________

____

Offender ______________________________

How he or she offended me ______________________________

____

How I responded ______________________________

____

Date I chose to forgive offender ______________________________

Action taken to rebuild relationship ______________________

____

Offender ____

How he or she offended me ___________________________

____

How I responded ____________________________________

____

Date I chose to forgive offender _______________________

Action taken to rebuild relationship ______________________

____

Offender ____

How he or she offended me ___________________________

____

How I responded ____________________________________

____

Date I chose to forgive offender _______________________

Action taken to rebuild relationship ______________________

____

Dealing with Guilt

20

Memorize: Romans 8:1–2; 1 John 1:9

When a person trusts Christ as Savior, the guilt of personal sin before God is forever removed. As far as one's standing with God is concerned, that individual is from that moment on unconditionally accepted and declared righteous by God, even though, as a new believer, he or she has a lot of personal weaknesses, hang-ups, and sins in his or her daily life for which victory has not yet been experienced. This perfect standing, free from any condemnation, is because of the work of Christ on the cross and Christ's merits, given as a gift to the believer's account.

Then why do we believers still feel guilt at times? One dictionary defines guilt as "the *fact* of having committed a breach of conduct, especially violating the law and involving a penalty . . . a *feeling* of culpability or blame." Notice there are two distinct parts—the *fact* of guilt and the *feeling* of guilt. They are not one and the same. The fact of guilt for us as believers exists whenever we have violated a clear statement or command of God's Word.

When we feel guilty, we need to ask ourselves, "Have I violated a clear statement or command of God's Word?" If we have not, then our feelings of guilt are based on erroneous information, sometimes rooted in false standards that are merely man-made. For instance, young children in elementary school often use the old saying, "Step on a crack, break your mother's back." Haven't we all felt an occasional twinge of guilt when we have stepped on a sidewalk crack? This is false guilt, of course, based on a foolish superstition. But if this standard is believed, it will produce the feeling of guilt. Is this guilt a *fact*? No. There has been no clear statement or command of the Word of God violated by stepping on a crack in the sidewalk.

But what if we do factually sin? Again we feel guilty, but this time the Holy Spirit can use these feelings to help reveal that he has been grieved. We are personally responsible for confessing our sins. God promises immediate forgiveness, and the fact of sin is then cleansed away. Accepting God's forgiveness because of the cross releases our feelings of guilt as well.

But what if our feelings of guilt remain when there is no longer any fact of guilt? That means we have not forgiven ourselves. We erroneously forget that the reason God forgives us is because of the cross. When we do not forgive ourselves, it means we are holding a grudge against ourselves. The motive for any grudge is vengeance. We look at ourselves as bad, even though God says we are righteous. We want to punish ourselves with penance of one kind or another.

Satan can be at work when we have feelings of guilt without any unconfessed factual guilt. He is the accuser of the brethren. He puts us down and makes us expect that God will cast us away if we sin. He makes us fear punishment, which is contrary to God's promises "for those who are in Christ Jesus" (Rom. 8:1). Satan can give us self-depreciating thoughts that make us feel unworthy of restored fellowship with God. He also gives us feelings of alienation and isolation from the very people who care most for us, and of course that includes God.

Feelings of guilt without the *fact* of guilt have no valid reason for existence. The woman at the well in John 4 was factually guilty of being with a man who was not her husband. She also had feelings of guilt, as evidenced by her obvious desire for isolation from the other ladies of Samaria. This woman came to get water when the other women would not be there. The Lord Jesus saved her, and the fact of her guilt was cleansed away.

We can see that this woman released her feelings of guilt also. No longer did she practice isolation. Instead, she lifted her head with confidence, returned to her village and spoke not only to the ladies but also to the men of her village, inviting them to come and meet Jesus for themselves. Some of these people may have called her names, but she now knew who she was on the inside. She was a new and clean person with a new life to live! She was in touch with a new feeling of self-worth because she believed the Lord Jesus.

Will you believe him? Your sins are blotted out if you have trusted him to be your Savior. Your standing with him is that of a righteous person. The past is not part of who you are now. Forgive yourself as God has.

Scriptures for Study

1. *Romans 8:1.* What does not exist anymore for the believer?

2. *1 John 1:7.* How broad is the cleansing for the believer?

3. *2 Corinthians 5:21.* When we trust Christ, we discover that a swap of sorts has taken place. What do we now have from God in our relationship to Christ?

4. *1 John 3:4.* Can you find a definition of sin in this verse?

5. *Mark 7:1–8.* What false guilt were the Pharisees trying to impose on the disciples? How did the Lord clarify the situation?

6. *1 John 1:9.* What is our responsibility in connection with any daily sins we commit as believers? What does the Lord promise to do immediately?

7. *Romans 4:5–8.* In verse 6, what connection does our own good works or efforts have to our righteous standing before God as believers? Since the above is true, can any personal failures and sins change our standing before God?

Personal Project

By completing the following phrases, examine three sins you have committed since you were saved. (If possible, include a Bible verse for "What God says about it.")

The sin itself ____

____

What God says about it ____________________________________

____

____

How I feel about that sin ___________________________________

____

How I obtained forgiveness for that sin ________________________

____

Date I claimed God's forgiveness and forgave myself ________

The sin itself ____

____

What God says about it ______________________________

____

____

How I feel about that sin ____________________________

____

How I obtained forgiveness for that sin _________________

____

Date I claimed God's forgiveness and forgave myself ______

The sin itself ______________________________________

____

What God says about it ______________________________

____

____

How I feel about that sin ____________________________

____

How I obtained forgiveness for that sin _________________

____

Date I claimed God's forgiveness and forgave myself ______

Additional Study

The Scriptures describe several things God does with our sins—blots them out like a thick cloud, casts them behind his back, buries them in the depths of the sea, removes them as far as the east is from the west (an infinite distance in contrast to north or south).

Look up as many of these references as possible in a Bible concordance. Read and list the verse and explain its significance to you.

Verse	God's Action Toward Our Sins	How Should This Make Us Feel?

Overcoming Inferiority Feelings

21

Memorize: Psalm 139:14; Ephesians 1:5–6

It is very natural for each of us to have struggles with inferiority feelings, and many of these feelings began when we were young children. Perhaps some well-intentioned but misguided person corrected us or made fun of us in such a way that we felt generally disapproved of—or at least embarrassed. Most of us also experienced teasing from our siblings or peers, and we probably did our share toward others as well. Children can sometimes be quite ruthless and cruel. We may remember being teased because of ears that stuck out more than some of our friends' ears, a nose that was shaped a little differently, legs that were somewhat bowed, or a body that was a little shorter, taller, or otherwise physically different from most of our schoolmates'.

How about you? Have you had similar experiences? But did you notice one thing—that inferiority is the result of comparing ourselves with others? God's Word tells us in many ways that such comparisons are unwise. We are created to be unique, not like anyone else. Just as our fingerprints are unique, everything else about us—our unchangeable physical characteristics and our inherent talents—is unique as well. God's Word says God prescribed every part of us while we were forming as a beginning human being in our mother's womb. The details about God's plan for us were written in God's design book in heaven. After we were formed, God threw away the blueprint. We are unique originals. That's the way God wants us, and he does all things well.

We were designed with God's purpose in mind, which was to magnify his Son through our lives in a very special way. Instead, we often find ourselves comparing ourselves with others and feeling inferior because we believe the lie that somehow we are less worthy as persons if we are not like most people—we don't look the same or are not as tall; we don't have as much money, as big a house, or as new a car; we don't have as great a mental capacity or as superior an athletic ability. As teens we especially felt the pains of inferiority. During the transition from being a child into being an adult, we felt awkward at times. Differences from our peers seemed more pronounced. Teasing was common.

Some of the ways people handle their feelings of inferiority can be described in an acrostic spelled ACTION.

A like-ism: "I can hide myself by being like everyone else. I must not be different in appearance and behavior."

C ompensation: "I'll find what I can do well and concentrate on it, whether it be sports or good grades or whatever. That way I will be accepted and respected for something."

T rip out: "It's impossible to make the pain go away, so I will hide in drugs and alcohol."

I ntroversion: "If I am a quiet little mouse, maybe no one will know I exist. If I open my mouth or take some initiative, I might make a mistake and people would laugh at me. I can't take the risk."

O bstinate: "I will pretend that I am tough and crude. I can bluff people into thinking I am confident by the way I show disrespect to others and treat them like trash."

N it-witty: "I will be a clown. I will do stupid things and make people laugh, especially at me. When they laugh, I won't let myself feel they are laughing at me for any reason other than because I make them laugh. I feel important when people are happy because of me."

Did you find yourself in any of those scenarios? Do you see that none of them is the answer? We will always have inferiority feelings at times, but growth into more self-confidence comes as we accept ourselves as unique persons designed by God to magnify his Son in our lives. This prayer may help you accept yourself just as you are—part of God's plan:

> Thank you, Lord, for the way you made me, the parents who gave me birth, the circumstances that were part of my life, the great lessons I have learned, and the opportunities I know are ahead as I exercise my faith and step out for you.

Scriptures for Study

1. *2 Corinthians 10:12.* What was the practice of some religious leaders in Paul's day that we should avoid if we want to reduce the tendency to feel inferior?

2. *1 Corinthians 4:3.* Instead of feeling inferior or intimidated by his critics, how did the Apostle Paul evaluate the importance of their words?

3. *Psalm 139:13–18.* What does this passage of Scripture tell you about the plan of God in designing who you are physically? Now praise the Lord by forming a thank-you prayer based on verse 14.

4. *2 Corinthians 12:7–9a.* Even with physical weaknesses or handicaps, believers can accept their situation if they have what Paul had, something that enabled him to bear up under it all. What was it?

5. *2 Corinthians 12:9b–10.* What were *two* special privileges connected to spiritual maturity that God was able to entrust to Paul while he was handicapped?

Additional Study

Moses was one of the most gifted individuals who ever lived (Acts 7:21–22). He had the best education available in Egypt—plus personal contact with the living God of Israel. Yet, at the age of eighty, he faced a significant struggle with inferiority feelings. For the following verses, list what Moses said that demonstrated his feelings of inferiority; how God responded to Moses' statement; and significant insights or applications for us as believers.

Exodus 3:11–12

What Moses said (v. 11) ______________________________

____

God's response: (v. 12) ______________________________

____

Insights and applications ______________________________

____

____

Exodus 3:13–14

What Moses said (v. 13) ____________________

____

God's response (v. 14) ____________________

____

Insights and applications ____________________

____

____

Exodus 4:1–9

What Moses said (v. 1) ____________________

____

God's response (vv. 2–9) ____________________

____

Insights and applications ____________________

____

____

Exodus 4:10–12

What Moses said (v. 10) ____________________

____

God's response (vv. 11–12) ____________________

____

Insights and applications ____________________

____

____

Exodus 4:13–17

What Moses said (v. 13) ____________________

____

God's response (vv. 14–17) ______________________________

____

Insights and applications ______________________________

____

____

Up from Depression

22

Memorize: Psalm 42:5; John 14:1

Depression is one of the most common emotional problems in our nation. It is also one of the most debilitating and serious disorders. Depression is sometimes described as an emotional shutdown. It is as if part of a person dies. There is a feeling of the blahs, a loss of energy and motivation, a generalized feeling of pessimism. There may be such symptoms as a change in sleep patterns, perhaps awaking early and being unable to go back to sleep. There may also be changes in appetite, a loss of confidence, and a sense of being overly self-focused.

Persistent depressed feelings can lead to what is called a medical or chemical depression, in which certain brain chemicals are actually depleted. This condition is dangerous and may be accompanied by thoughts of suicide. That is why it is extremely important for a seriously depressed individual to check with a Christian psychiatrist or at least a family physician immediately. Anti-depressant medication may be prescribed to give temporary relief until counseling can begin to take place.

Depression is a signal that there are other problems in one's life. When certain emotions are produced but are not expressed in a healthy manner, they become blocked and turned inward. These may include grief over a real or imagined loss; anger that is unresolved; exaggerated anxiety, guilt, or loss of self-worth; as well as other possible emotional pain. Often the depressed person's self-talk is negative about his circumstances, depreciating toward himself, and seemingly hopeless as far as his future is concerned. There may be a perfectionistic attitude that underlies the problem, which sets up almost certain failed expectations of self and of others.

Careful and usually long-term counseling is needed to deal with unresolved emotions that have been turned inward. At our clinic we refer to this as insight-oriented counseling because it helps the counselee gain an understanding of why he feels the way he does and what can be done about it. In our experience, such counseling invariably succeeds when the counselee cooperates with the counselor. There is definitely hope for the depressed individual.

The most common root problem we have noted for depression is anger turned inward. If you are depressed, can you identify the angry feelings you may have? Your counselor will want you to verbalize these feelings in order to help break up the emotional logjam. Grudges will need to be released, vengeance turned over to God, and forgiveness granted to offenders. Self-worth issues usually also need to be discussed, and your personal view of self will be enhanced as you gradually see yourself as a worthwhile person to God, to others, and to self.

Commitment to action is often a necessary part of recovery from depression. Action taken to revitalize a regular spiritual life is a good first step. This should include learning how to worship and praise God every day. In fact, we have found that what Howard Hendricks describes as "the therapy of thanksgiving"—listing, acknowledging and giving thanks for specific positive things in our lives—can function as a tremendous antidote for depression.

Another action step involves committing to a physical-exercise plan. Exercise helps produce the endorphins that are lacking in the depressed person. It is also important to build a relational life—getting out of the house or out of the rut, meeting people, talking, sharing and developing friendships.

Finally, a lifestyle of ministry helps in the recovery process. The counselee is activated into serving others on a practical level, seeking to minister to the needs of another person at least once a week. This can include visiting someone in a hospital or nursing home, writing a note of appreciation to someone who has been a blessing in the past, or sharing one's growing personal optimism with a discouraged friend.

The depressed person's tendency toward self-preoccupation can gradually become refocused with the proper guidance. Joy and perspective will return as depressed individuals receive help in understanding their emotions and accepting their own worth and then see God's expression of love in their outreach to others in need.

Scriptures for Study

1. *Psalm 42:3–4.* How would you describe the psalmist's emotional state at this time? If you have ever felt this way also, what were the circumstances?

2. *Psalm 42:5–6.* How is the psalmist turning his feelings into words? Clue: He is verbalizing by talking out his feelings to ________________ (v. 5) and to ______________ (v. 6). Because we are reading his words, we can assume that he probably committed his feelings to what other form?

3. *1 Peter 1:18–19.* From these verses, how can you determine your true personal worth to God?

4. *1 Kings 19:4.* Which symptoms of depression can you identify in Elijah's life from this verse?

5. *1 Kings 19.* What gradual corrective steps were provided for him from the following verses?

(a) vv. 5–6
(b) vv. 10–14
(c) vv. 15–16
(d) v. 19

Personal Project

Moses, David, and Jonah also sometimes became depressed. Look at the following passages and ask yourself these insightful questions.

Numbers 11:10–15

Who became depressed? ______________________________

Under what circumstances? ___________________________

____

Why depressed? _________________________________

____

How depressed? _________________________________

____

Significance to me ______________________________

____

____

Solution for depression ___________________________

____

Jonah 4

Who became depressed? ______________________

Under what circumstances? ______________________

____

Why depressed? ______________________

____

How depressed? ______________________

____

Significance to me ______________________

____

____

Solution for depression______________________

____

Psalm 32

Who became depressed? ______________________

Under what circumstances? ______________________

____

Why depressed? ______________________

____

How depressed? ______________________

____

Significance to me ______________________

____

____

Solution for depression ______________________

____

Facing Fears and Anxiety 23

Memorize: Psalm 56:3–4; Philippians 4:6–7

Anxiety is probably one of Satan's most effective ways to keep people in a form of bondage. Christ came to deliver those who, through fear of death, were subject to slavery all their lives (Heb. 2:15, NASB). "Fear of death" can relate to either fear of physical death or fear of the death of self-worth—a loss of personhood. Sometimes we fear the death of self-worth more than we fear bodily death, injury and disease, or the loss of someone who is close. Each, in its own way, can cause us to believe certain circumstances will destroy us.

Anxiety is a feeling of dread, apprehension, or uneasiness that results when we fail or refuse to look at our hidden motives or emotions. It equates to a sense of approaching danger from an unknown or unreasonable cause, it is inappropriate fear.

That means, of course, that there is such a thing as appropriate fear and concern. Appropriate fear is a protection system God has given us. It signals us when we get too close to the edge of a cliff, when we are near people who have a contagious disease, when we are in a car traveling at excessively high speed, or when we are physically threatened by another.

In situations of actual danger, the body's defense mechanisms are activated by the sympathetic nervous system, and we are energized for action. This "fight or flight" preparation includes such physiological changes as elevated blood pressure, higher heart rate, and increased blood sugar. When the danger is past, these functions return to normal.

Inappropriate fear—anxiety—on the other hand, includes fear of failure, rejection, disapproval, put-downs, criticism, and so on. Anxiety means we are trying to reach into the future to control it, thus playing God. Furthermore, anxiety will produce the same kind of physiological response as appropriate fear.

The Greek word used for anxiety means to be distracted or divided in mind, to be drawn mentally in different directions. Anxiety is a distracting emotion, an unrealistic fear that paralyzes us and prevents us from doing God's will. It calls forth the same bodily responses needed for protection in actual threatening situations, but the "danger" seems ever-present.

Most anxieties have two components, according to William Backus. One is a negative prediction; the other is a negative distorted evaluation. For example, you worry that a person you think is special will totally reject you (negative prediction). You believe that such a rejection would be unbearable (negative evaluation).

Ninety percent of the things we worry about do not come to pass. Even if some of them do, they would be stressful or painful, but certainly not unbearable. Since God promises not to allow testings to come to us that we cannot bear, the evaluation is usually distorted.

These types of negative thoughts help create anxiety. The first step is to identify the issues that can rob us of the peace of mind we should enjoy. Sometimes, especially if there is unresolved guilt or anger in our subconscious mind, the Holy Spirit may be bringing the issue up into our awareness so it can be dealt with. Because of our reluctance to see ourselves as less than perfect, we push it back down. This struggle can produce anxiety.

Once the specific cause of your anxiety has been identified—and counseling is often needed for this—a useful plan by which people have been helped to overcome anxiety involves positive praying, linked with positive thinking, followed by positive action. *Positive praying* includes thanking God in advance for how he will work this issue out for your good and his glory. For example: "Dear Lord, I am anxious about my job interview next week. Give me calmness and sharpness of mind, and I am thanking you in advance for how you are going to make this situation work out for my good and your glory."

Positive thinking trains your faith to look realistically and through the eyes of God's promises at each potential cause of anxiety. Instead of the "what ifs" of negative prediction, think on the "as ifs" of positive faith. "Faith cards" can be made—with positive answers, including Scripture, to both the negative prediction and the distorted and pessimistic evaluation.

Positive action considerably reduces anxiety. Paul confidently announced: "I can do all things through Christ which strengtheneth me" (Phil. 4:13, KJV). Anxiety is desensitized by choosing to take small steps forward into the very thing you fear. Using the example of the job interview, step one could be to practice introducing yourself in the mirror, then on a tape recorder, then to a close friend, and then finally to the prospective employer. Learning how to talk to yourself internally about what action you will take and telling yourself to relax and stay cool are also helpful devices when facing times of stress.

The result of dealing properly with anxiety will be peace of mind. "Peace" is not necessarily the absence of conflict, since there will always be stressful situations to face. But, for the believer, it can be defined as a sense of adequacy in Christ, even in the face of conflict.

Scriptures for Study

1. *Hebrews 2:15.* What is the emotion Satan has effectively used in robbing people of the freedom and wholeness God wants them to enjoy?

2. *2 Timothy 1:7.* The kind of fear that blocks us from doing God's will does *not* come from where?

3. *Matthew 6:30–31.* Observing the last phrase in verse 30 and the first phrase in verse 31, what is lacking in our thinking processes when we are anxious?

4. *Philippians 4:6–9, 13.* A three-step plan for dealing with anxiety is suggested by the apostle Paul in these verses. Can you identify each step?

    Verse 6
    Verse 8
    Verses 9, 13

5. *Philippians 4:7.* What is the blessing we experience when we deal biblically with our anxieties?

Personal Project

One of the most significant passages on anxiety is Matthew 6:25–34. Pick out a key word or phrase for each verse. On the basis of this develop a practical insight or application. Then write a summary statement for the entire passage.

Matthew 6:25

Key word or phrase ______________________________

Practical insight or application ______________________________

____

____

Matthew 6:26

Key word or phrase ______________________________________

Practical insight or application ______________________________

____

____

Matthew 6:27

Key word or phrase ______________________________________

Practical insight or application ______________________________

____

____

Matthew 6:28

Key word or phrase ______________________________________

Practical insight or application ______________________________

____

____

Matthew 6:29

Key word or phrase ______________________________________

Practical insight or application ______________________________

____

____

Matthew 6:30

Key word or phrase ______________________________________

Practical insight or application ______________________________

____

____

Matthew 6:31

Key word or phrase ______________________

Practical insight or application ______________

____

____

Matthew 6:32

Key word or phrase ______________________

Practical insight or application ______________

____

____

Matthew 6:33

Key word or phrase ______________________

Practical insight or application ______________

____

____

Matthew 6:34

Key word or phrase ______________________

Practical insight or application ______________

____

____

Summary Statement ______________________

____

____

____

Resolving Grief

24

Memorize: Isaiah 53:4–5; Romans 5:3–5

Grieving is experiencing an emotion described as pain, distress, or sorrow. In *Called to Counsel,* Timothy Foster writes that grief is usually associated with the loss and sadness we feel when someone or something in which emotion has been invested has been taken away. The Lord Jesus showed grief by weeping at the grave of his friend Lazarus. The Holy Spirit is grieved when we resist his leadership in our lives. The people of the church at Thessalonica were grieved by the loss of some of their loved ones through death. Their grief was especially vivid in light of their uncertainty about the participation of their departed ones in God's prophetic plans, about which the apostle Paul had taught them. We note that Paul did not ask them *not* to grieve over their departed friends, but rather not to grieve to the extent and with the despair of people "who have no hope" beyond this life (1 Thess. 4:13).

Grieving is a proper emotional experience, one which needs to be expressed. Covering up or repressing your grief is not a sign of spirituality but an unhealthy choice that could lead to long-term depression. You may feel overwhelmed by grief over the loss of a loved one, the loss of a relationship, the loss of a job, the loss of your health, the loss of self-respect, the loss of faithfulness on the part of your spouse, or some other loss. A Christian counselor can help you get in touch with your feelings and work through the following generally predictable stages of grief reaction:

1. *Denial.* The individual refuses, momentarily or for a time, to believe what has happened.
2. *Anger Turned Outward.* This is an angry reaction toward someone other than oneself. That stage almost always includes some anger toward God for allowing the loss to occur. After accepting the reality of both the loss and the angry reaction toward God (or whoever else is held responsible), the grieving person begins to feel guilty. This leads to the third stage.

3. *Anger Turned Inward.* This anger directed at oneself is generally a combination of false and legitimate guilt and is usually worked through fairly quickly. If a grieving person stays longer than a week or two in this stage, the grief may become a clinical depression that could take months to work through in therapy.
4. *Genuine Grief.* This is vitally necessary in the healing process. An individual who suffers a significant loss should definitely have a good cry.
5. *Resolution.* This is almost automatic, once the other stages have been worked through. During the resolution, one's zest for life and joy are gradually regained.

Some authorities identify the five stages of grief by other terms and slightly different sequence. For example, first there could be *denial*—"There must be some mistake." The denial stage may be a defense mechanism for handling the shock. Then comes stage two, which is *anger.* There may be many targets for a grieving person's anger—including God. Next comes the *bargaining* stage, which is most evident when a loved one's death (or your own) seems imminent. Many vows are made to God in the emergency room or while preparing for a serious operation. It seems easier to face the loss, or its probability, if we are trying to do something to help. The fourth stage, *depression,* is reached when one's energy and resources have been exhausted by anger and bargaining efforts. Finally, the last stage of *acceptance* is reached when the promises of God's Word produce a confidence and trust in God's wisdom and love.

Sad times will come back for the individual who has suffered a loss, but they last for significantly shorter periods of time and become less frequent as time goes on. Grief feelings lessen in intensity as positive possibilities begin to occupy more of the heart and mind.

Scriptures for Study

1. *John 11:33–36.* As you observe the example of the Lord Jesus Christ in this passage, what conclusions do you reach about the philosophy of some people who say, "Snap out of it! Don't cry; Don't be emotional. Christians should always be happy." Or "Grown men don't cry"?

2. *1 Thessalonians 4:13.* If the apostle Paul was not discouraging grief in the loved ones of some who had died, what attitude was he urging them to adopt as they experienced their grief?

3. *Psalm 13:1–5.*

Who was the psalmist angry with?

Are you ever angry in the same way?

To whom is the psalmist verbalizing his anger?

Is his method one you could use?

Since we are reading about his feelings, he must have used an additional method. What was it?

Could you follow his example and work through this stage of grief?

4. *Romans 5:3.* What positive resolutions are suggested in this verse for a person who goes through tribulations?

5. *Romans 8:28–29.* What should we know with confidence about the final goal of God as he meets us in our trials?

Additional Study

Since grief is so often connected with death, the following Scriptures can give us additional insights about what the Bible teaches on the subject of death. For each of the following passages, give the teaching or truth explained and the significance or application for the believer. (Use the first reference as an example.)

2 Corinthians 5:6–8

Teaching For the Christian at death, his or her soul/spirit immediately enters the Lord's presence.

Application There will be no "soul sleep" for the Christian, but at death we immediately enter the presence of the Lord.

John 10:10; John 14:1–4

Teaching ______________________________

____

Application ______________________________

____

____

2 Samuel 12:15–23; Matthew 19:13–14

Teaching (about death of children) ___________________

____

Application ___________________________________

____

____

Job 7:8–10; Hebrews 9:27

Teaching (about reincarnation) ____________________

____

Application ___________________________________

____

____

Philippians 1:20–24

Teaching _____________________________________

____

Application ___________________________________

____

____

1 Corinthians 15:50–52

Teaching _____________________________________

____

Application ___________________________________

____

____

Psalm 116:15

Teaching ____

____

Application ____

____

____

Isaiah 57:1–2

Teaching ____

____

Application ____

____

____

25 Overcoming Suicidal Tendencies

Memorize: Jeremiah 29:11; 1 Corinthians 6:19–20

One of the major symptoms of depression is painful thinking, which usually includes ruminating over one's own past mistakes or worrying over real and imagined wrongs inflicted by others. When a negative self-concept already exists, self-blame is applied to all a person's problems, which results in that person feeling blue, sad, helpless, hopeless, worthless, empty, and utterly alone. Painful thinking overrides one's motivation, so that activities once enjoyed lose their appeal and there seems no way to find pleasure in life.

Other effects of depression include avoiding people and a desire to be alone. There is also loss of a sense of humor, an inability to make decisions, and the emergence of suicidal thoughts. These death thoughts are very dangerous since they can quickly snowball into a definite plan, which can lead rather quickly to an attempt at suicide, even for one who under normal conditions would never believe such thoughts were possible.

The apostle Paul was concerned about a man who had apparently suffered the loss of his privilege to associate with his fellow Christians because of an arrogant practice of publicly known sinning. Although the man had evidently repented, the danger now was that the believers would not see the importance of welcoming him back into their support and fellowship. Paul said, "Now instead, you ought to forgive and comfort him, so that he will not be overwhelmed by excessive sorrow" (2 Cor. 2:7). There would be a serious problem for this man if the believers did not soon offer their acceptance and support.

Suicides are committed by people in all age brackets from young children to the elderly. Today, suicide among teenagers is a definite cause for alarm. However, the suicide rate is higher among the divorced, widowed, and upper socioeconomic groups. It is most common among single, white, adult males over forty-five years of age. Several warning signs that alert a counselor to suicidal tendencies include intense feelings of hopelessness, the experience of a significant loss, such as death of a spouse, breakup of a marriage, or loss of a job. Also involved may be an individual's intense need to achieve.

It is important for the suicidal person and his or her loved ones to plan immediate remedial steps to counteract the self-destructive thoughts and behavior. If you harbor such feelings, share them with your family and contact a trusted friend, counselor, or pastor for outside help. This will be no time for covering up or trying to maintain an image of strength. Pray together and let others bring you comfort, reassurance, and hope-filled Scripture. If your depression is severe, psychiatric treatment and even hospitalization may be needed.

When a believer is able to think through his convictions, it is instructive and sometimes healing to consider God's will concerning suicide. Christians regard suicide as a sin equivalent to murder, since "Thou shalt not kill" applies to a person's own life as well as the lives of others. Of the seven suicides recorded in Scripture, none of the perpetrators was in the will of God. Although a Christian who commits suicide would not lose or jeopardize his eternal salvation, to take one's life deliberately is to commit an act that is expressly forbidden by God and would grieve him deeply.

Emotional suicide precedes the physical act. A person may set himself up for self-destruction by attaching all feelings of worth and purpose for living to something transitory or someone who could be taken away. As believers, we should wrap our lives around the Lord, since only he is permanent and can never be taken away from us. Emotional suicide involves getting into a distorted mind-set where you believe you could not bear to live if a certain person did not approve of or love you or if some other factor in your life were altered from what it appears to be in the present.

If you are suffering this type of emotional pain, here are some good questions to think through. If you died and came back to life, could you find other reasons for being glad to be alive? Would the Lord's promises of love and guidance through your trials still be in place? Would the sun still shine and water still be cool and refreshing? Would there still be adventures in life and growth in relationships? Could some positive reasons for living, as opposed to dying, be developed? Yes, yes, a thousand times yes! There is hope for the hopeless!

A certain Southern preacher delivered a sermon on "And It Came to Pass." His point was that our trials and troubles always come to *pass;* they don't come to *stay.* Wait patiently with hope! Hang in there! Remember, too, that suicide is a selfish step that puts many additional burdens on the very ones you love. There are wonderful children or parents or friends to whom God has called you to minister. They need you. God never rescinds his call on your life. He asks you to be a good soldier of the cross and will give you the strength you need.

If you are dealing with another individual who you believe is experiencing thoughts of suicide, talk to that person compassionately, but don't be afraid to bring up the subject of suicide. Ask such questions as: "Are you thinking about taking your life? Do you have a suicide plan as to how you would do it? Why do you think that's the only answer?" Kindly, but straightforwardly, encourage him to discuss his feelings and present reasons for him to go on with his life.

In contrast to the thinking of some people, raising the subject does not plant suicidal thoughts in the mind of an already depressed person. From our years of counseling experience we have concluded that these thoughts are, in every instance, already in place. Talking about suicide actually helps decrease the possibility that the individual will actually take his life.

Another positive step is to try to obtain a verbal "non-suicide contract," a commitment not to do anything that would be harmful or self-destructive without first talking with you or with a counselor, pastor, or another trusted individual. We know of many instances in which compassionate friends, relatives, or loved ones have raised the question and thereby actually saved the life of an individual who was considering suicide.

Scriptures for Study

1. *1 Kings 19:1–4.* Here the prophet Elijah heard from God in a time of despair. What kind of painful emotions can you identify in Elijah?

2. *Matthew 27:3–5.* Was Judas in the will of God when he committed suicide? What would have been a better option?

3. *2 Corinthians 2:7.* What kind of support does Paul suggest for a person in danger of being overwhelmed by sorrow?

4. *James 5:16.* What methods are suggested in this verse for spiritual and emotional healing?

5. *Psalm 43:5.* What word describes the psalmist's solution to his despair? With whom was this solution linked?

Additional Study

In each of the following passages, identify the individual who committed suicide. Then determine whether he was a believer; whether he was in God's will; the circumstances leading to the suicide; and the evidence of demonic or satanic activity, if any (compare John 10:10a and John 8:42–44). Finally, list any practical lesson to be learned from each individual's story.

1 Samuel 31:1–7

Individual ______________________________

Believer? ______________________________

In God's will? ______________________________

Circumstances ______________________________

____

Evidence of demonic activity ______________________________

____

Lesson ______________________________

____

2 Samuel 17:1–23

Individual ______________________________

Believer? ______________________________

In God's will? ______________________________

Circumstances ______________________________

____

Evidence of demonic activity ______________________________

____

Lesson ______________________________

____

Matthew 27:3–5

Individual ______________________________

Believer? ______________________________

In God's will? ______________________________

Circumstances ______________________________

____

Evidence of demonic activity ______________________________

____

Lesson ______________________________

____

Avoiding Workaholism 26

Memorize: Matthew 11:28–29; Mark 6:31

An addiction is a compulsion that takes over control of one's life. Workaholics have become addicted to their profession or business. Their self-worth is fed by the significance they feel as they pursue their driving lifestyle in the workplace. Lack of balance is a description of their lives. The workaholic's priorities are often upside down or otherwise distorted. The obsession of his life (and this could be "her," of course) is business or work and its associated meetings, luncheons, committees, seminars, or other activities. It could be a pastor's church that takes on this obsessive quality. Similarly, some Christians' ministering projects so overwhelm their lives that they crowd out other normally healthy and scriptural responsibilities to family and self. The workaholic can often be described with words like these, used by Chuck Swindoll: "We worship our work, work at our play, and play at our worship."

Some symptoms of workaholism are as follows: starting a job but having no peace until it is finished; becoming so preoccupied by a thought that we cannot get it out of our minds; having periods in which we cannot sit or lie down because we need to be doing something; a belief that the person who works the hardest and longest deserves to get ahead; feeling uncomfortable as a student unless we are getting the highest grades; frequently feeling angry without knowing what or who is bothering us; always wanting to be in control of our circumstances and other people in our lives; expecting things of ourselves that no one else would ask of us; desiring that others see us as not having any faults; and having few close friends with whom we share warm feelings openly.

The four signs of a workaholic are:

1. *A schedule that is usually frantic.* A fourteen-hour (or more) workday is not unusual. The workaholic is often trying to do two or three things at once, packing far too many events or items into a schedule of activities.

2. *Conversation about one's work or accomplishments.* It seems a workaholic needs to prove to others he or she is worthwhile through personal achievements. Others never hear about a spouse or family unless it is in the context of how the workaholic is providing or working hard for them.

3. *An inability to say no.* The workaholic often is motivated by a need for approval from others. Whatever it takes to maintain that approval seems to be the workaholic's creed.

4. *An inability to rest or relax.* A workaholic's lifestyle is one that often leads to cardiac or circulatory problems. Even in quiet moments or on vacation, the person is thinking about work. Workaholics hardly ever take time to be alone with loved ones, to be quiet, to meditate on God, or even to watch television without being obsessed with catching the various newscasts that might relate to their work. Even when time is taken for relaxation, a workaholic will usually be combining it with reading or working on professional literature or papers.

There are many adverse effects on the marriage and family life of a workaholic. For example, a wife frustrated by her inability to have a normal relationship with her husband, due to his extreme preoccupation with productivity, may invest herself totally in her home life to the exclusion of everything else. Or frantic social activities may be pursued in order to meet her need for intimacy. If either plan fails to meet her personal needs, she becomes angry and frustrated and ultimately depressed. The children of workaholics may become depressed, too, or engage in destructive acting-out behavior to gain attention. Many incidents of teenage pregnancy, suicide, eating disorders, and juvenile delinquency are by-products of workaholism in one or both parents.

The workaholic is best described as an obsessive-compulsive personality. He or she is a perfectionist whose unrealistic standards can often be traced back to an overly critical and negative environment in childhood, or at least to a lack of positive reinforcement.

If you are a workaholic, there are several ways you can begin to turn things around. First, make sure you have trusted Christ as your personal Savior. This includes understanding that God's grace gives you worth and acceptance totally apart from your works of merit. If you truly accept your position in Christ, you will have the security to also accept personal failures, ineptness, and humanness as part of your experience as a normal, growing believer.

The next step is to commit your life totally to Christ and to the Word of God, which should be the overriding standard and guide for all you do. This means putting God *first,* giving him top priority by setting aside time to worship him, study his Word, and pray on a regular basis. Commitments to other people and even to yourself must always be ranked lower in importance than your relationship with God. Next on your priority list should be your marital and family commitments, which are infinitely more important than your commitments at work, even work done for the church. If you consider attending to your spouse's needs as a God-given mission, you will easily see that spending time alone with your wife or husband is vital for achieving the mutual sharing that marks a healthy marriage. Your children, too, deserve your undivided attention frequently. Be there for them when they require loving discipline, but also plan periodic family fun times and try to have a special "date" with each child at regular intervals.

Only when you have fulfilled your responsibilities to God, to your marital partner, and to your children are you free to turn your attention to your professional life. Although this is a necessary investment of time, it is but one part of your personhood and should be curtailed whenever higher-priority items place demands upon your time. Finally, you must realize that no one's life is completely whole without an outlet for fellowship in church, recreational, and/or community activities. Find time, too, for personal relaxation in whatever pastime gives you solitary pleasure, whether it be reading, exercising, or a special hobby.

The prescription for the workaholic is balanced living. With these guiding principles, your days will be lived in accordance with God's will, and you will find new insight into the words of the Lord when he said, "Come to me. . . . For my yoke is easy and my burden is light" (Matt. 11:28, 30).

Scriptures for Study:

1. *Luke 10:38–42.* Which one of the two women in this passage was probably attaching her self-worth and security to what she did rather than who she was?

2. *Luke 10:41.* What emotion does the Lord Jesus identify in Martha that fueled her behavior?

Do you think that emotion was related to a defense against being criticized, a fear of appearing lazy, or a method she had learned for gaining approval?

3. *Matthew 11:28–30.* If verse 30 describes the Christian life as it is generally experienced, what conclusions can you reach about the percentage of tasks in a constantly overinvolved person's life that actually originates from God's will?

4. *1 Timothy 5:8.* What application of this verse can be made to your own life? *Clue:* Consider whether your job or even your Christian service has had a higher priority in your schedule than you have made for the needs of your spouse and your children.

5. *John 2:1–11.* From verse 11 we see that this event was Christ's first miracle in his earthly ministry. He was thirty years of age. Seeing many needs and having the power to meet those needs was regulated by his top priority, which was submission to *whose* will?

How would that priority regulate your life and the ability to say no?

Additional Study

Examine Mark 6. List the events that influenced the workers in the verses listed on the next page and the lessons to be learned for workaholics.

Verse	Principle Expressed	Application or Insight for Us
7–11		
12–13		
14–29		
30		
31a		
31b		
32		
33		
34		
35–36		
37–44		
45		

27
Beating Burnout

Memorize: Isaiah 40:31; Lamentations 3:22–23

Closely associated with workaholism is one of its common side effects: burnout. This term has a counterpart in the technological field, where burnout of a jet engine simply means "cessation of operation." No doubt you know someone, perhaps yourself, to whom this description could apply, since we can experience burnout in our occupation, within our family or marriage relationships, or even in our Christian life and service.

One of the most common definitions of human burnout describes it as a loss of enthusiasm, energy, idealism, perspective, and purpose. The symptoms of burnout include emotional exhaustion, a desire to withdraw from people, and an increasing inability to function or perform. Burnout can be viewed as a state of mental, physical, and spiritual exhaustion brought on by continued stress. Yet there is hope. Burnout is often short-termed, especially if it is understood and corrective steps are taken.

Some stress in a person's life is to be expected and, in fact, can be a positive factor in motivation. But too much stress over too long a period of time can result in burnout. When the burnout is severe and not alleviated by learning and applying certain coping techniques, it can lead to depression.

Burnout is more likely to happen to people involved in serving the needs of others rather than to those receiving the service. For example, it often occurs in mothers of small children or in doctors and nurses, schoolteachers, pastors, missionaries, social workers, police officers, and administrators in related fields. It is most likely in environments where there is more negative feedback than positive, more unacknowledged service than appreciation and thankfulness.

If you have "burned out," the people in your life often are seen in a negative focus—as problems, rather than as individuals whose needs and feelings are exciting projects and challenges. "The world would be a nice place if it were not for people," is the type of self-talk message that points to burnout. Unfulfilled expectations are present in the lives of most burnout victims.

Even though many of our expectations are unrealistic, we make unwritten rules on how people should act and relate to us. The trouble is that we become angry when people break our rules. Bitterness is the hidden root of burnout. Bitterness is unresolved anger that is allowed to intensify and fester in one's heart. It is usually associated with the belief that the object of our anger has deliberately deprived us of the fulfillment of a basic need necessary to our own self-worth. This bitter resentment may be our response to what we perceive as unfair treatment or demands, or a lack of recognition by others whom we consider significant in our lives.

How can the experience of burnout be avoided or reduced? Keeping the proper perspective in your work and relationships is a good beginning point. God calls us to minister to others' needs as a Christian obligation, not for the sake of gaining their approval. It is okay to want approval but not if we need it in order to function. As believers, we do have God's approval up front, and that is what we need. It is normal to desire approval from other people, but safer not to expect it. If it does not come, then there are no unwritten rules broken to cause you to become angry or bitter.

Another step is to commit yourself to a balanced priority system for your lifestyle, as outlined in the previous chapter. Occasional breaks for diversion and laughter are necessary to break up the sometimes frustrating routine during the course of a day. Weekend outings and scheduled vacations to different locations of interest are beneficial in restoring mind and body. (There is good reasoning behind some employers' *requirement* that all their personnel take time off for an annual vacation.)

Other suggested balancing factors include pursuing a hobby and developing a support system of positive-minded friends you can associate with regularly. It is also important to exercise at least three times a week (for twenty minutes or more each time), eat a balanced diet at regular mealtimes, and get close to eight hours of sleep each night. Try to eliminate the unnecessary "shoulds," "musts," and "oughts" in your self-talk. Above all, practice forgiveness toward others and yourself and share your feelings with your spouse or a close friend. And develop a sense of humor! The TV program "M.A.S.H." is an example of people under prolonged stress who coped with burnout by injecting humor into their circumstances.

Let's turn down the heat and turn back the burnout.

Scriptures for Study

1. *Acts 13:6–13.* Does John Mark's return to Jerusalem in verse 13 indicate a possible burnout in light of the stress mentioned in the previous verses?
2. *Romans 15:29–32.* Paul faced exposure to antagonistic people during his missionary journey. What resources for coping can you see in these verses?
3. *Hebrews 11:24–27.* Moses chose to suffer affliction with the people of God. Can you identify several methods he used for successfully coping?
4. *1 Corinthians 6:19–20.* Since our bodies are God's temples, what do you think our attitude should be about caring for them? In what ways can we practice a good maintenance program for our bodies?
5. *Mark 6:31.* How could these instructions of the Lord to his disciples be applied to your life as a preventive measure against burnout?

Additional Study

One of the most significant examples of burnout in Scripture is Elijah. First look for some reasons for Elijah's burnout and then identify the steps God took to reverse burnout in this prophet's life. (Follow the example in the first two references.)

1 Kings 18:1–13 (example)

Reason for burnout Elijah's life had been threatened by Ahab because of his fulfilled prediction that there would be no rain (vv. 1–2).

Significance to us When under intense and continual pressure, even men of God are susceptible to burnout.

1 Kings 18:17–39

Reason for burnout Elijah's intense confrontation with 450 prophets of Baal, during which his life and reputation were on the line.

Significance to us ______________________________

____

1 Kings 18:46

Reason for burnout ______________________________

____

Significance to us ______________________________

____

1 Kings 19:2

Reason for burnout ______________________________

____

Significance to us ______________________________

____

1 Kings 19:5–6

What God did to reverse burnout ______________________________

____

Significance to us ______________________________

____

1 Kings 19:7–8

What God did to reverse burnout ______________________________

____

Significance to us ______________________________

____

1 Kings 19:9

What God did to reverse burnout ______________________________

____

Significance to us ______________________________

____

1 Kings 19:11–13

What God did to reverse burnout ______________________________

____

Significance to us ______________________________

____

1 Kings 19:13–14

What God did to reverse burnout ______________________________

____

Significance to us ______________________________

____

1 Kings 19:15–18

What God did to reverse burnout ______________________________

____

Significance to us ______________________________

____

1 Kings 19:19–20

What God did to reverse burnout ______________________________

____

Significance to us ______________________________

____

PART 3

Becoming a Whole Person

This next section of what we might call a "maturity manual" will deal with some ideas about reaching the full potential God intended for you—as a believer and also a productive member of society. "Achievement" in any undertaking requires first that we understand our place in the grand scheme of the universe (see Part One). Next, we must be able to deal with our emotions (see Part Two). For believers, it also means placing just about everything we do in the context of God's will and timing for our lives. Within that framework, we "live and move and have our being . . ." (Acts 17:28).

In the process of daily living, we are challenged to make sometimes-difficult choices and solve a variety of problems, both large and small. The way we tackle these assignments is colored by our personal convictions, even as we draw upon the strength God provides through a wide range of resources. We will examine the foregoing aspects of "whole personhood" in this section, hoping that you thereby gain a more complete picture of how to attain a healthy self-concept as a unique child of God.

Understanding Our Feelings

28

Memorize: Psalm 42:11; Philippians 4:8

In surveying the negative emotions discussed in the previous section—and how to turn them around—it becomes obvious that feelings are a very important part of our lives. Many people come to counselors because they are puzzled and sometimes frightened about their feelings. "I wish I could understand my emotions," some say. Others ask, "If I don't like my emotions, how can I change them?"

The first thing to learn about analyzing our emotions is that we cannot control them directly. The reason is that they are side effects of something else that we *can* directly command, namely our thoughts. The thinking process that causes our feelings involves our beliefs, which we internally recite to ourselves in what is called "self-talk." Therefore, feelings cannot be classified as good or bad. They are only signals of our present self-talk. Emotions are like a smoke alarm, faithfully responding to the stimuli of the beliefs we are using as we evaluate each circumstance.

Some research indicates that we talk to ourselves at the rate of approximately 1,300 words per minute. According to David Stoop, in *Self Talk,* we normally talk to others at the rate of approximately 180 words per minute. What we believe is partially determined by the programming we absorb from our early childhood up to the present. Our parents, siblings, peers, teachers, significant others, books, TV, and so on, all contribute to our perceptions about the world and ourselves.

It is possible to learn to rigorously challenge old misbeliefs as we gain insight into truth. After we trust Christ, we are illuminated by the Holy Spirit to understand more and more of the Word of God, which sanctifies and transforms our behavior and feelings as we renew our minds on a regular basis. We thus learn to evaluate each circumstance with beliefs and self-talk that look at the larger picture of God's purpose and love in everything. We call this "faith-oriented self-talk."

Dr. Albert Ellis describes the ABC's of our emotions as follows: "A" stands for the *actuating events* in our lives (our environmental circumstances) and "C" refers to the *consequential feelings and behavior.* Our common misunderstanding is that "A" equals "C," but that is not the true picture, since one factor is missing. The "B" in the equation refers to our *beliefs*, which we recite in our self-talk as we evaluate "A" and read a meaning into it. That combination—"A" plus "B" equals "C" (our feelings)—gives us the total picture.

Negative emotions are often related to distorted thinking. We can change our emotionally dysfunctional reactions to each circumstance by discovering our distorted misbeliefs, challenging them vigorously, and replacing our evaluational self-talk with truth- and faith-oriented self-talk.

One event in the Israelites' history was facing a giant named Goliath. As they prepared to do battle with this formidable enemy, the feeling among the armies of Israel was paralyzing fear. Young David came along and evaluated Goliath in a faith-oriented way that resulted in feelings of strength and confidence.

How could the same circumstance cause two contrasting kinds of feelings? The answer is the differing "B's" in the equation. The Israelite forces believed they would fail. David believed in God's power and said in his heart, "The Lord . . . will deliver me from the hand of this Philistine" (1 Sam. 17:37a). David applied faith-thinking to his circumstance. His success-oriented belief and self-talk about the actuating event caused his confident feelings. "For as he thinketh in his heart, so is he . . ." (Prov. 23:7, KJV).

Some irrational misbeliefs that may be the source of a lot of disturbed emotions are:

"It is necessary for me to be loved and approved by others."

"I must always be perfect in my achievements and above criticism in order to be worthwhile."

"I cannot help the way I feel."

"Because I am a Christian, God will not allow negative things to happen to me."

"My feelings are always a true sign of God's love, presence, and guidance."

"God can't use me unless I am spiritually strong."

Challenge the misbeliefs that are stifling your life! Replace them with the reality of the promises in God's Word. As Jesus told us, "Then you will know the truth, and the truth will set you free" (John 8:32).

Scriptures for Study

1. *Acts 16:25.* In their very difficult circumstances of having been beaten and thrown into jail, what was the form of self-talk chosen by Paul and Silas to give a broader meaning to their situation?
2. *Psalm 15:2.* What kind of self-talk does the psalmist say is used by the man who dwells in fellowship with the Lord?
3. *Philippians 4:11.* A feeling of contentment was not automatic for Paul. What word describes the discipline necessary for him to develop contentment, whatever the circumstances?
4. *Psalm 42:11.* Here the psalmist chose faith-oriented self-talk. What spiritual quality was he challenging himself to accept as he looked at his situation?
5. *Hebrews 12:2.* What was the mental focus the Lord Jesus chose in enduring the cross?

Additional Study

Keep a journal of stressful situations and your reactions for a period of time, using the chart below. In the first column, list the stressful situation. In the second column, record what you are saying to yourself about the stressful situation. Later, in the third column, see if you can argue against the negative thought in the second column and replace it with a broader, more positive perspective.

Stressful Situation	Automatic Negative Thoughts	Positive Faith-Oriented Countering Thoughts
1.		
2.		
3.		
4.		
5.		

Basic Personal Needs — 29

Memorize: Mark 12:29–31; Philippians 4:19

If we are to be able to function in a responsible way in our daily environment and relationships, we must know that certain needs are being met in our lives. Beyond our basic physical needs for food and shelter, there are intangible necessities without which we are not completely fulfilled as human beings. These "personal" needs are intimacy with God, fellowship with other people, and self-worth. Another way of describing our personal needs is that we must have unconditional love and acceptance, a feeling of being cared for, and a lifestyle that makes an impact on others with good and lasting effects. Our self-worth is enhanced to the extent that those emotions and qualities define our lives.

Yet another way of describing these basic needs is that we need a sense of belongingness, an assurance that we are considered worthy by someone important to us, and a feeling that we are useful and competent. When I believe that someone important to me wants me and accepts me, I can regard myself as "good," approved, capable, and adequate to deal with daily life, partly to satisfy that person.

Dr. Lawrence Crabb, Jr., says that each individual must have a valid way to regard himself as a person of personal worth. This is in place and functioning when two basic needs are met: the need for security and the need for significance. Throughout the ages, it has appeared that women have needed more security than significance and that men have emphasized "significance." Some would dispute this generalization, but it may be one reason that God instructed husbands to love their wives and wives to submit to their husbands. "Love" contributes significantly to one's sense of security, and respect, or "submission," contributes to another's feeling of significance. *Security* includes being able to regard ourselves as loved, accepted, and cared-for as individuals. *Significance* involves being able to regard ourselves as important and valuable to others in impacting their lives for good.

These two basic needs were met for Adam and Eve through their capacity to enjoy fellowship with their Creator in the Garden of Eden. When they sinned against God, however, their fellowship with him was broken. Among other consequences of the fall was the disruption of their capacity—and ours—to enjoy security and significance in relationship to God.

Each person among us comes into this world with a vacuum in his or her soul. From childhood on, we seek to fulfill our unmet needs through our parents, our siblings, our peers at school, our teachers, and other authority figures. As adults we feel special affirmation from a loving marital partner, but the search goes on throughout life. To some degree we find the fulfillment of our personal needs in our relationships with specific people, and there is nothing wrong with that. However, sooner or later we discover that they, too, are human: their love and acceptance are conditional. Since their care for us has limitations, we sometimes feel insecure and insignificant.

Then how can our needs for security and significance be met? We learn from the Word of God that God created man for himself. Because he seeks our fellowship and loves us, he has provided a way for our reconciliation. When we trust Christ as our Savior, we are reunited into a relationship with God that is even closer than the one enjoyed by our first earthly parents, Adam and Eve. As we become identified with Christ, God sees us and accepts us unconditionally in Christ's name. We are at this moment loved, accepted, and cared for by the most important being in the universe—God, our Creator and loving Father.

Our lives then take on new importance, touching others with his love in such a way that the impact of what we do will last for all eternity. All our personal needs are met by God through our relationship with his Son, the Lord Jesus Christ, by whatever means he chooses to use. Even when we feel rejected or inadequate on the human level, we can train our faith to believe the abiding truth that we are secure and significant in Christ. We can therefore continue to function in a responsible, loving way, and we can release others from the expectation that they have to be the primary source of the fulfillment of our personal needs. God shall supply all our needs (Phil. 4:19)—in Christ we have been made complete (Col. 2:10).

Scriptures for Study

1. *Mark 12:29–31.* The responsibilities cited in these verses are three-dimensional. Can you list the three objects of love? (Two are stated directly; one is implied.)

2. *John 17:23.* Here the Lord Jesus prayed that the world would someday know how much God the Father loves all believers. In what ways have you seen how much your Father in heaven loves you?

3. *Ephesians 1:18.* Who makes up God's inheritance? Does this mean we are considered valuable to God?

4. *Philippians 4:19.* Who is the ultimate source of fulfillment for our needs?

5. *Ephesians 2:10.* How does this verse show that God has an important purpose for your life?

6. *Matthew 6:25–34.* What emotion does the Lord not want us to feel, in light of his loving goodness and care over our lives? What is the strategy for daily living mentioned in verses 33–34?

Personal Project

Examine the following passages. Determine what they say about your significance as a person. Then list or write any personal applications or insights you have gained from examining these passages.

Passage	Significance	Personal Application
Matthew 6:26–30		
Romans 12:3		
1 Corinthians 12:12–26		
Ephesians 2:10		
Psalm 139:13–16		

Additional Study

What do the following passages have to say about belonging, worth, and competence?

Belonging

Romans 8:15–17 ______________________________

____

____

Ephesians 1:3–6 ______________________________

____

____

Worth

John 10:27–30 ______________________________

____

____

1 John 3:1–3 ______________________________

____

____

Competence

John 16:7–15 ______________________________

____

____

Romans 15:13 ______________________________

____

____

30

Decision Making and God's Purposes

Memorize: Proverbs 15:22; James 1:5–6

One of the greatest privileges we have as humans created "in the image of God" is the ability to make choices. God has given us the freedom to exercise our will. Of course, we are ultimately accountable to God for the decisions we make, and this is a serious responsibility. Since this is true—and also because we love and trust our Creator—it is obviously to our advantage to solve our problems and make our decisions in a way that is harmonious with God's purpose and timing. Even relatively minor decisions (such as what to order from a restaurant menu) are not always easy to make, and at times we are overwhelmed by the importance of the problems we face and the choices to be made in the process of solving them.

The purely practical aspects of what is called "problem solving" in psychology texts, do-it-yourself manuals, and management handbooks generally revolve around the basic steps needed to reach a given outcome. For example:

1. State your desired goal (and there may be transitional subgoals to be reached en route).
2. Identify the obstacles to be overcome in attaining that goal.
3. Gather all pertinent information.
4. List the available options, including the pros and cons of each.
5. Plan the course of action or make a specific decision, if such is needed. As you weigh the relative merits of the options and eliminate those with more negative than positive overtones, you will reach a potential solution to the problem (that is, how to reach the goal). If there seems to be more than one acceptable option and you can test each of them in the actual situation, fine. However, this is often not possible.
6. Execute your plan or decision, modifying some of its details if you discover some unexpected obstacles or new information along the way.

That kind of problem-solving approach has the best chance of bringing success as you reach for a given goal. However, a believer will also want to have the assurance that the goal itself and the means for reaching it meet with God's approval. Making the effort to discover God's will may be difficult when you are operating as part of a group or where a spur-of-the-moment decision is required because of professional or business considerations. However, we, the authors, recommend the following approach to decision making whenever possible, especially when your course of action has personal significance and/or affects the loved ones for whom you are responsible. This plan, as you will see, can be integrated into the problem-solving steps already outlined. It involves discovering God's will for the matter at hand by asking yourself five questions before finalizing any important decision:

1. *"What does the Bible tell me to do?"* This is where you determine God's moral directive. God gives us all a great deal of freedom in choosing—*except* when we attempt to move outside the circle of his moral law. If your choice of action would violate God's Word, you know God's will in the situation: "Don't do it!" Only if your tentative decision would not violate God's Word are you free to proceed. The matter then becomes one of "fine tuning," being sensitive to the leading of the Holy Spirit, who will bring more information to your mind, especially relevant principles and examples from the Scriptures. This is the first part of gathering information—knowledge that will give you the wisdom to make the best choice from two or more alternatives.

2. *"What can God show me as I pray?"* Even when you are convinced that your tentative decision or plan would not be a sin, you will want further guidance through prayer. For example, suppose you are contemplating relocation to another state and need some direction on whether this would be a wise move. You have already determined, after searching God's Word, that such a move would not violate any scriptural command, but now—on the basis of James 1:5—you commit yourself to pray for God's leading every morning for two weeks. At the outset, you could prepare a sheet of paper on which are drawn two columns, one for listing all the reasons you can think of for making the move, and the other listing reasons why you should not. Each evening, you cross off a reason on one side or the other, as a result of what God told you during your prayer time that day. At the end of the two-week period, you should see a definite

trend developing, especially if you have continued to study God's Word and scriptural aids. (This process, you will note, has certain similarities to Step 5 in the previous problem-solving plan, in that you are actually comparing the pros and cons of one or more "options.")

3. *"What can knowledgeable counselors or advisors tell me?"* According to the Book of Proverbs, seeking appropriate guidance from others can bring wisdom, safety, and a better chance of success. This, too, has a parallel in the first plan (Step 3), except that here the information you "gather" is on both the practical and spiritual level.

4. *"What do these circumstances tell me about God's purposes and timing?"* Here you are asking whether the existence of this situation (and thus the need to make a decision) tells you something about God's plan for you. For example, is he showing you that some doors are now open? Are other doors being closed?

5. *"Is my heart filled with peace about my decision?"* This is a very subjective question, which is why we have saved it for last. According to Colossians 3:15, "the peace of Christ" is an important element in our fulfillment of God's will in our lives. If your decision is "right," you will feel great confidence, not only that you had God's approval for the choice you made, but that your "fine tuning" to God's many sources of wisdom worked to your advantage in this situation and will continue to do so. A decision that is in the will of God will bring you "success," though not necessarily according to the world's standards. In fact, you may reach, not the specific goal toward which you were striving, but an even better one.

What decisions are you facing? What secret goals do you want to attain, yet have been too timid to try for them? Take the responsibility right now for discovering solutions and making appropriate choices. If your aspiration is in God's will for you, he will help you reach it—but first you must seek his leading and then follow his road map, which will get you where you want to be.

Scriptures for Study

1. *Romans 14:12.* How does this verse indicate that each of us is responsible for the decisions we make in life?

2. *1 Corinthians 6:12.* According to the first part of this verse, why is there a need to "fine tune" our decisions, even if we know that what we plan to do would not be morally wrong?

3. *James 1:5–6.* What source of wisdom for understanding what God is doing in our lives is suggested by verse 5? In using this resource, what does verse 6 tell us about the necessary attitude we should have?

4. *Proverbs 11:14; 15:22; 24:5–6.* What other source of information or guidance is suggested by these passages to help in our problem solving or decision making?

5. *Acts 16:6.* How else does God show us what is—or is not—his will and reveal his timing, as suggested by this verse?

Additional Study

Complete this chart, showing (1) what each passage tells about God's will and timing, and (2) how you could apply this teaching to your life.

Passage	Teaching	Application
John 7:17		
Romans 15:32		
Ephesians 6:6		
Philippians 2:13		
Colossians 4:12		
1 Thessalonians 4:3		
1 Thessalonians 5:18		
Hebrews 13:21		
James 4:15–16		
1 Peter 2:15–16		

1 Peter 4:2		
1 John 2:17		

Personal Project

We have already discovered the passages in Proverbs (11:14; 15:22; 24:5–6) that point to the benefits of obtaining pertinent information and advice from other human beings when faced with a problem to solve or an important decision to make. On a separate sheet of paper, describe a problem or decision you recently faced. Next list the specific advisors (if any) you consulted at that time. Finally, list other sources of facts or guidance that might have added to your success if you had consulted them in this situation.

Forming and Practicing Convictions

31

Memorize: Romans 14:14; 1 Corinthians 6:12

There are many squabbles between believers over ethical issues—what is right or what is wrong for the Christian. In thinking about this subject, there are some definitions we need to make and some dangers we need to point out. The Bible states that each believer is a spiritual priest and has direct access to God. This results in the freedom of each believer to follow the Holy Spirit's leading in making choices in life situations whenever a clear statement of the Word of God is not thereby violated. This liberty, of course, is always within the framework of loyalty to the lordship of Christ and the authority of the Word of God.

The opposite of Christian liberty is called "ethical legalism," which was the practice of the Pharisees during Jesus' earthly ministry. They made their own rules, interpretive conclusions, and preferences stand as moral law for everyone, measuring people's spirituality by these man-made rules and traditions. "Pharisees" (and there are still many around today) have a right to form their own convictions about certain ethical matters, but not to give their convictions the force of God's law as found in the Bible, nor to impose them on others. We have heard of entire congregations splitting over issues as trivial as open-toed shoes, women wearing slacks, or similar issues. In like fashion, some marriages develop conflicts to the point of separation over questions about the morality of watching TV, wearing makeup, eating pork or shellfish, or choosing a certain hairstyle.

We have found it helpful to categorize our convictions into three levels, according to their source and therefore their degree of importance in a believer's life:

1. *Clear Bible statements or commands.* This includes scriptural directives that unquestionably carry the force of God's authority,

such as the command to love and forgive others or the prohibitions regarding adultery, stealing, lying, drunkenness, and so on. We who are committed to the Word of God must live by its clear-cut principles and must do our best to convince others to do so as well.

2. *Personalized Bible interpretations.* Here are convictions that a believer has reached by studying the more ambiguous scriptural passages and drawing his (or her) own conclusions as to their meaning. Although an individual will not compromise such convictions in his own behavior, he will realize that others equally committed to the Word may interpret certain portions of the Bible differently and therefore reach different conclusions as to the ethically correct behavior. At this level, a believer would not ostracize or even criticize another believer because of these differences of opinion. Instead, while holding fast to his personal convictions, he recognizes that Christian liberty allows others to make choices according to their conscience. For example, some believers (in fact, entire denominations) believe that divorce is never permissible for a Christian, regardless of the circumstances, and therefore that remarriage after divorce is not allowable in the eyes of the church. Recognizing that other sincere believers have interpreted the Bible differently on the matter of divorce, those in the first group are called on to respect the second group's convictions and the right of an individual in that group to act accordingly.

3. *Personal preferences.* These are convictions that develop as a result of family tradition, geographical considerations, cultural background, or simply individual taste. In these areas, a believer will not only be respectful of another's right to a different viewpoint (as in #2) but will be open to the possibility that there may be some merit in the other's preference. Even if he does not change his own opinion, a believer is ready to yield momentarily so that Christian love and forbearance can have a positive outflowing. For example, when a suggestion is made to change the format and content of a traditional Sunday-morning service, there is sometimes opposition within the congregation by those who are convinced that the old ways are the only ways acceptable to God. In fact, they are judging the merit of the suggestion only on the basis of their own preference, rather than on a Bible-based directive. In such a matter, a Christian is expected to be open to giving the other point of view a chance. He might even find that his own taste is changed!

Most squabbles between Christians and divisions in churches are over issues that relate to categories two and three. In the area of ethics, we believe that when other adult believers who are committed to the Word of God make choices in their lifestyle that do not violate clear Bible statements—even if they differ from our own convictions—we should refrain from comments or attitudes of censorship. I am free to share my interpretations and personal preferences with you, but I must not insist that these conclusions carry the authority of God's law upon you or other believers. My leadership in these areas will not be by censorship, demands, or intimidation, but by the logic of my conclusions and the example of my life.

Satan likes to use certain individuals to control the lives of others in the name of spirituality, in order to redirect the emphasis of the Christian life away from Christ and toward the externalities of man-made rules. This game plan marks out those who could more easily be identified as on *our* side. Let us not fall into this divisive trap.

To put all of this together in the context of personal experience, we have developed an acrostic using the word *STAND* as a guide for forming and maintaining our personal convictions.

S criptures are not violated (1 John 3:4).

T ake the side of right as opposed to the side of evil (Rom. 12:9).

A ffirm the leadership of the Holy Spirit (Rom. 8:14).

N ever move toward personal enslavement (1 Cor. 6:12).

D etermine the effects on another believer (Rom. 14:21).

Do you have such a plan for sorting out your values and convictions?

Scriptures for Study

1. *Galatians 5:1.* According to this verse, what is our important responsibility when other people try to impose their personal convictions on us, making them a false standard of spirituality?

2. *1 Corinthians 6:9–10.* Are the behaviors listed in these verses clear Bible statements of wrong behavior?

3. *1 Corinthians 6:19–20.* If a man uses these verses as a basis for not eating pork, is that his privilege? (*Clue:* Is a clear Bible statement at issue or a personal interpretation?)

4. *Galatians 6:12.* According to the apostle Paul in this verse, what was the real motive behind the attempt of some leaders to get others to follow their interpretations of spirituality?

5. *Romans 14:5.* According to the last part of this verse, what is the important thing to consider when it comes to making ethical choices about which the Bible has made no clear statement?

Personal Projects

1. *Clear Bible statements or commands.* Describe several of your strongest convictions in this category, including a pertinent Scripture reference for each. For example: "I must abstain from immorality" (1 Thess. 4:3), or "I must choose to forgive" (Eph. 4:26–32).

____

____

____

____

____

2. *Personalized Bible interpretations.* Describe several of your convictions in this category, including at least one scriptural basis for each. For example: "I should have devotions in Scripture daily" (Ps. 1:2; Josh. 1:7–8), or "I should take occasional time off for rest and recreation, setting aside one day each week for a change of pace that should include a time of worship" (Mark 6:31; Acts 20:7; 1 Cor. 16:2).

____

____

____

____

____

3. *Personal preferences.* Those who are relatively new to Bible study and the Christian life often find it frustrating to learn that everything is not "black or white." For example, although 1 Corinthians 8 can help us develop principles for relating to others, the teachings are broad enough to allow for variations in our behavior and attitudes.

Ask yourself the following questions: How do I maintain balance? How do I deal with legalistic individuals or individuals who overstress liberty? If no one is looking, can I do what I please? Is there anything I am presently doing that I should give up or stop doing? What kind of Christian am I? A weaker brother, a legalistic Christian, a balanced individual, a libertarian? Use the chart below as you study the Bible passages indicated.

Scripture Passage	Key Thought	Application(s) for My Life
1 Cor. 8:1–6	Principle of liberty	1. My behavior should be motivated not by self-indulgence but rather by a love for fellow Christians. 2.
1 Cor. 8:7–13	Principle of love	1.

32

Developing a Healthy Self-Concept

Memorize: Romans 12:3; Ephesians 1:3–5

We all carry a mental description of ourselves. That picture determines whether we like ourselves and can celebrate who we are or—on the contrary—dislike what we see about ourselves and do not feel comfortable with the individuals we are. This self-concept affects our relationships with other people, how we deal with trials and how we see the purpose of our lives. A self-concept is healthy when it reflects valid reasons to regard ourselves as people of personal worth.

Some common symptoms of a poor self-concept are over-defensiveness, difficulty in accepting compliments and love, inappropriate behavior or emotions when rejected or embarrassed, an addiction for approval, a strong fear of criticism, and/or paralyzing fear of failures.

Our self-concept was first painted for us as children by our parents and others significant to us. Their love (or lack of it), attention, words, and attitudes reflected to us who we were. For example, a certain five-year-old boy who was usually a little terror in his Sunday-school class showed a transformed behavior one Sunday. The child had won a contest and was crowned king for a day. He strutted around the classroom with dignity in his kingly cardboard crown and cloth cape, graciously acknowledging the homage by his classmates. What changed his behavior, even if it was for only one hour? It was his changed self-concept. He saw himself as a king and thus worthy of respect!

Our behavior and feelings are usually consistent with beliefs about ourselves. When the apostle Paul began his letters to various churches, he identified *who* he was, *what* he was, and *why* he was. *Who?* Paul. *What?* Among other things, an apostle of Christ. *Why?* "By the will of God."

How would you identify yourself by these same criteria? It seems we assign to various significant people in our life the role of mirroring our identity back to us. If they say that they love us or that we are good, competent, and so on, then we feel good about ourselves. We feel worthwhile. However, when these mirrors, for whatever reason, reflect negative information such as criticism or rejection, we will feel worthless, unless we have a strong inner source of personal worth and identity. This inner source is the privilege of every believer.

Once we have trusted Christ as Savior, we have the opportunity to define ourselves in a brand-new way. This is done by allowing God to mirror back to us through his Word *who* we are when we identify with Christ. Each of us is created in God's image, and each of us is unconditionally loved.

As an unconditionally accepted person, you are the object of God's care. Your worth is not related to your works or achievements but to your belief in who you are—a person redeemed by the blood of the Son of God. You are also the temple of the Holy Spirit. God lives in you and has a personal relationship with you! You are a jewel in God's hand. You are an heir to God's kingdom and a joint-heir with Jesus Christ! Since he is "King of kings" and considers himself your elder brother, you are in that sense a member of the royal family. You have an important mission to fulfill every day; God has chosen you to be his ambassador. You are a spiritually gifted person, placed in the body of Christ as a channel through which the Lord's love can flow to touch another's life, making an eternal impact on that person by your example and words.

Yes, you are special to the most significant being in all the universe, the Triune God! Let God's Word erase your negative self-images of the past, your feelings of worthlessness. Let your faith become trained to remind you who you really are in Christ—a person who is loved and belongs, who is worthy, and who is competent to do God's will and fulfill his purposes, one day at a time.

Scriptures for Study

1. *Proverbs 23:7.* According to this verse, what is the key internal process that affects a person's behavior and feelings? (*Clue:* See especially the King James Version.)
2. *1 Corinthians 1:1.* What three things does the apostle Paul tell us about his self-concept in this verse?

3. *Romans 6:6.* How should we regard our history of past sins, once we have trusted Christ as our personal Savior?
4. *Romans 6:11.* How should our identity with Christ govern our day-to-day behavior?
5. *John 17:23b.* How deeply does God love us, according to this passage?
6. *Ephesians 1:4.* What phrase in this verse assures you that God wanted a personal relationship with you before you ever wanted him in your life?

Additional Study

One of the most significant passages in Scripture on self-concept is Romans 12:3. Many of you have memorized Romans 12:1–2. In preparation for this assignment, work on memorizing Romans 12:3. Divide the passage into phrases, as below. (These are from the King James Version.) List the significance of each phrase in regard to self-concept. Be sure you understand the meaning of "soberly" in this context.

"For I say, through the grace given unto me,"

Significance for self-image ______________________________

____

Application ______________________________________

____

"to every man that is among you,"

Significance for self-image ______________________________

____

Application ______________________________________

____

"not to think of himself more highly than he ought to think;"

Significance for self-image ______________________________

____

Application ____

____

but to think soberly,

Significance for self-image ______________________________

____

Application ____

____

"according as God hath dealt to every man the measure of faith."

Significance for self-image ______________________________

____

Application ____

____

PART 4

Growing in Relationships

How we relate to others provides a means of both measuring our emotional maturity and motivating our further growth in Christ. Since the way we treat other people—whether they are family, close friends, or mere acquaintances—reflects the way we regard the Lord (Matt. 25:31–46), we can be assured that he uses us to bless others, just as he uses others to bless us. The way we handle our relationships can also signal whether or not our faith is holding up (James 1:26–27). Similarly, our ability or inability to love others—which is what relationships are all about—confirms or denies our professed love for Christ (1 John 3:23–24).

This section will begin with a survey of "love," .its different meanings and how to manifest each type of love appropriately. Several chapters are devoted to the closest human relationship: marriage. We discuss the importance of communication in marriage and outline how God's purpose is to be fulfilled in the complementary roles of husband and wife. Since the closer the relationship the deeper the potential pain it can bring to one or both parties, there are words of advice here for handling a spouse's adultery, dealing with divorce, and adjusting to the death of your marriage partner. There are also chapters addressing "co-dependency" and the need to forgive our parents for real or imaginary past wrongs.

Through our relationships, we are challenged to learn more about ourselves, including how to express our emotions effectively and when to surrender them to God instead. As we learn to accept ourselves because of God's unconditional love for us and forgive others because he forgives us, we will become more mature in handling our feelings. The result will be more meaningful and stable relationships.

The Nature of Love

33

Memorize: 1 John 3:18; 1 John 4:10–11

God *is* love, and his Word says that love is *from* him. Just as God loves us, so also ought we to love one another. The greatest challenge in the Bible is twofold: "Love the Lord your God with all your heart and with all your soul, and with all your mind, and with all your strength" *and* "Love your neighbor as yourself." Love is to permeate all our relationships. Love should fill the very atmosphere of our homes and marriages: "Husbands, love your wives, just as Christ loved the church and gave himself up for her" (Eph. 5:25).

Let us look at "love" from three different perspectives. There are three Greek words that can be used to identify these three kinds of love.

The first is *eros.* This is emotional love. Although it is based (at least in part) upon physical attraction, it is enhanced by touching and hugging in nonsexual ways. Of course, in marriage, *eros* includes romantic sex. This kind of emotional love is very important to the marital commitment and is described by such words as "satisfy" and "exhilarated" in the Book of Proverbs. If *eros* is neglected in a marriage, Satan will come knocking at the door with his temptations. Each partner in the marriage should nurture this kind of love by kissing, hugging, compliments, eye contact, provocative teasing, romance, and so on.

When married people say they have "fallen out of love," *eros* is usually what they are talking about. It can be rekindled when such damaging emotions as unresolved anger, anxiety, or guilt are removed. Sometimes the absence of *eros* in a marriage means that it has been invested in a third party, even if only on an emotional level. Even in a good marriage, it is not uncommon for romantic love to be greatly diminished for a short period of time if the pressures of work and the weariness of the human frame are overwhelming. This kind of love needs constant nourishment and investment of affection.

A second kind of love is *phileo.* This refers to relational love, which means being best friends, doing things together, giving high priority to time together. In a marriage, it might include developing shared hobbies, going on "dates," taking weekend excursions together. It basically involves sharing each other's lives—playing games, watching a TV program, remodeling a room, bowling, fishing, camping, relaxing, laughing, planning, praying, reading the Word, and going to church.

This kind of love could be defined as delight in another's presence. It is nurtured by communication and developing common interests. The Bible, in Titus, uses the Greek word *philandros,* from the same root as *phileo,* when it talks about a woman's love for her husband. This refers to relational love. In a marriage, it means being best friends, doing things together, and giving high priority to time together.

The third kind of love is *agapē.* Since this love is mental and volitional, it is the most important kind of love and operates by obedience and faith. Here we see the commitment phase of love. It is not merely a feeling but a choice to act in a caring way for another. *Agapē* love is defined as taking the kind of initiative to meet real needs in another's life that will result in their spiritual growth. *Agapē* injects strength into both *eros* and *phileo.* It is the word used in Ephesians where the man is called upon to love his wife.

This kind of love involves caring more for the other person than you care for yourself. In marriage, it is behaving lovingly toward your spouse, whether or not you feel like it and whether or not he or she responds positively toward you. *Agapē* love is motivated by spiritual commitment, not necessarily by feelings. It is nurtured by one's daily spiritual life with God.

Some ways to show *agapē* are as follows:

Say, "I love you"

Show appreciation and gratitude

Give compliments

Remember special occasions such as birthdays and anniversaries

Say things to others that cast your lover in a favorable light

Be gentle, considerate, and polite

Be helpful in sharing the chores

Make up little surprise notes or poems

Call home from work once in a while to say "hi"

Take time for the one you love

Restrain any tendency to be negative, judgmental, and self-centered

Love comes from God. We are able to love unselfishly once we are aware that we, too, are loved. It is because of God's love given to us that we have a lot of love to give to others. (See next chapter for more on *agapē*).

Scriptures for Study

1. *1 John 4:7.* This verse identifies the source of true love and also the kind of people who are called to show this love to others. Identify these two factors.

2. *2 John 5–6.* In these verses, the apostle John indicates that genuine love is not without boundaries of right and wrong. What is the standard for expressing genuine love?

3. *Proverbs 5:18–19.* From the last part of verse 19, identify a word that relates to *eros*-type love in a marriage relationship.

4. *Titus 2:3–5.* Wives were to be taught to love (philandros) their husbands, according to verse four. How would you explain what that means, especially to a young wife of our generation?

5. *Revelation 2:3–4.* As you study verse four, what three steps can you identify for reclaiming *agapē* that would apply to a marriage that needs a revival of genuine love?

Additional Studies

1. For each of the following Scriptures, first determine the kind of "love" involved. Then list at least three things you will do to enhance this aspect of love in your marriage or other relationships.

Ephesians 5:25–33

Kind of "love" ______________________________

Three things to enhance the love ____________________

____

____

____

Titus 2:3–4

Kind of "love" ________________

Three things to enhance the love ________________

____

____

____

Proverbs 5:18–19

Kind of "love" ________________

Three things to enhance the love ________________

____

____

____

2. Each of David's relationships could be characterized by one of the three words for "love": *agapē, phileo,* or *eros.* Look up each reference and identify the kind of love you think it was. Then consider whether it was appropriate (or inappropriate) and what was done or needed to strengthen it.

David and Bathsheba *(2 Samuel 11–12)*

Kind of love ________________

Appropriate? ________________

Done or needed to strengthen it ________________

____

David and Jonathan *(1 Samuel 18–20)*

Kind of love ________________

Appropriate? ________________

Done or needed to strengthen it ________________

____

David and Mephibosheth *(2 Samuel 4:4; 9:1–12; 21:1–7)*

Kind of love ______________________________

Appropriate? ______________________________

Done or needed to strengthen it ______________________________

____

Agapē Love

34

Memorize: Matthew 5:43–44, 1 Corinthians 13:4–7

This chapter will deal exclusively on the form of love identified in the Greek language of the New Testament as *agapē.* This kind of love is the greatest mark of spirituality a believer can have.

When the apostle Paul wrote his inspired letters to different churches in the New Testament period, he often praised them on their progress in spiritual growth. He did not measure their success by how many were in church on Sunday or how large was their offering. Instead, he usually assessed their spiritual growth by three qualities: faith, hope, and love. "Faith" was their growing relationship to God. "Hope" involved their response to life's circumstances because of that relationship. And "love" described their relationship to one another. Of these three, Paul said that love was the greatest quality—perhaps because it is *God's* love that forms the basis for the other two.

Agapē love can be defined in several ways. It is first of all a deep concern for the well-being of the loved one. But it is more—it is a volitional *choice,* a determination to act on behalf of that person. This earnest desire for the other's well-being, and an active and beneficial interest in helping achieve it, reflects a clear function of will and judgment. *Agapē* is an act of the will. It means taking the initiative to meet real needs in another's life, hoping that the individual will be a better person and have a richer life because of our love.

This is the kind of love God has for us. He chose to love us. He chose to take the initiative before we ever loved him, to act on our behalf, to meet our real need—the need for a Savior to redeem us from sin. His love gave. He gave sacrificially. He gave his Son. We who have trusted Christ as our Savior have the source of that love within us. As we yield control of our lives to the Holy Spirit each day, he expresses the "fruit of the Spirit" through us, qualities that start with *agapē* love for others (Gal. 5:22).

In 1 Corinthians 13, the apostle Paul describes some of the things *agapē* is and is not:

1. Love is slow to lose patience. It enables you to accept a difficult situation and wait upon the Lord to accomplish his will in his own good time.
2. Love looks for kind ways to neutralize another's harshness.
3. Love is not jealous or possessive. Because your security of being loved is based upon your relationship with Christ, his love in you enables you to grant freedom to another to love you only if *they* want to.
4. Love is not arrogant. It does not allow you to be filled with inflated ideas of your own importance. Rather, it helps you to express a servant's heart.
5. Love is not motivated by the applause of peers. It enables you to have the energy and inner purpose to say and do what is right, regardless of another's approval or disapproval.
6. Love is not rude, but shows good manners and respect.
7. Love is not demanding of its own "rights." It helps you to yield advantage to the person loved.
8. Love is not hypersensitive or easily hurt.
9. Love does not review wrongs already forgiven.
10. Love does not delight in another's failures.
11. Love is loyal to truth and right. It helps you to put Christ first when choosing the manner in which you will express love.
12. Love has the ability to live with the inconsistencies of others. It enables you to accept the fact that all humans make mistakes. *You* will make mistakes—and so will the one(s) you love.
13. Love lets you believe the best about a person, rather than accepting malicious gossip.
14. Love is hopeful. It injects you with unquenchable optimism in every direction.
15. Love has the power to endure difficulties. It enables you to rest upon your faith that God is in control of your circumstances.
16. Love's endurance remains, even in sickness, poverty, misunderstandings, and failures.

How do you rate your spiritual growth on the basis of those qualities of *agapē* love? Don't be discouraged. Resolve now to grow in this kind of love. The most effective witness to the world is how believers relate to each other in love. It is love that turns things around. It is love that releases bitterness and revenge. It is love that turns a house into a home, and it is love that gives us an opportunity to make an eternal impact on others with our lives.

Scriptures for Study

1. *1 Thessalonians 1:3.* What were the three qualities that Paul looked for when he wanted to measure the spiritual growth of believers?
2. *1 Corinthians 13:13.* Of the three qualities listed here, which one is described as the greatest?
3. *Romans 5:5.* According to this verse, who supplies God's love in us and through us to others as we yield to him?
4. *Matthew 5:44.* How does this verse show that *agapē* is not a feeling first, but rather an obedient choice of the will?
5. *John 13:35.* What does the Lord Jesus say is a practice by which believers could make the best impression on the watching world?

Additional Study

One of the key teachings about agapē love is found in 1 John 3 and 4. For each of the following references, list both the insight it gives about love and a practical personal application.

1 John 3:10–11

Insight ______________________________

Application ______________________________

____

1 John 3:14–15

Insight ______________________________

Application ______________________________

____

1 John 3:16–19

Insight ____

Application ____

____

1 John 3:23–24

Insight ____

Application ____

____

1 John 4:7–10

Insight ____

Application ____

____

1 John 4:11–14

Insight ____

Application ____

____

1 John 4:17–18

Insight ____

Application ____

____

1 John 4:19–21

Insight ____

Application ____

____

Help for the Husband

35

Memorize: Colossians 3:19; 1 Peter 3:7

It is interesting to discover that the word *husband* is an Old English word that means "to band together the home." Certainly the Christian husband must band together his marriage with love in order to accomplish his divinely appointed mission.

A proper marriage brings two people into a team relationship. Both persons willingly give up certain rights in order to gain certain privileges that belong to them in the marriage. One of the rights given up is the right to be a totally independent person. As a two-member team, they can function effectively only if they respect each other's particular role in the operation of the team.

A role is defined as a behavior pattern that is expected from a holder of a particular status. A football team assigns various roles to its members. For example, the quarterback calls the signals and throws the passes. The offensive lineman throws blocks to protect the quarterback. The place kicker is only called upon for a field goal or point after a touchdown. A defensive back is the last line of defense between the opposing team and his own goal line.

Likewise, marriage is based on a biblical plan for the flow of leadership and decision making. The two extremes on this subject are the macho marriage and the equalitarian model, but neither fulfills God's guidelines for a husband-wife relationship.

The "president-vice president" marriage—some call it the democratic model—is a balanced approach, more in line with such passages as Ephesians 5:21–33 and 1 Peter 3:1–7. There is freedom of both parties in sharing ideas and making decisions together under normal circumstances. However, when an impasse is reached, the husband holds 51 percent of the voting stock.

Let's look at it another way. The president of the team is the husband. He is called the *head* of the wife in the Bible. That role means he has the last word and is ultimately responsible to God for the decisions made within the marriage.

Howard Hendricks says the husband is also the *heart* of the home. He leads, but always with a loving concern for the welfare of his wife and family. He respects his wife as the executive vice-president. She is his helpmate, which means that the president does need help! He should encourage her freedom to express her feelings on any subject, even if they are contrary to his position. A husband can consider himself a man of wisdom only if he makes his choices based on the best information available, which may come through his wife. He should never have to feel intimidated by having a good researcher as his V.P.

Even the President of the United States needs help as chief executive. He has a cabinet of key people who search out the best information and options. Only if the President uses their wisdom and considers their advice can he function as a wise decision-maker. This, too, is teamwork.

In describing a man qualified for leadership in a church, the apostle Paul describes this role as that of a "manager." He delegates responsibility, always sensitive to the strengths and weaknesses of the team members. Likewise, a husband is to utilize the gifts and abilities of the entire family team. He is expected to carry the heavier load of being the primary breadwinner, setting policy for discipline of the children, and generally enforcing the plan of operation. He honors his wife as the physically "weaker" and more delicate vessel. A good husband relates sexually only to his wife and lives joyfully with her. He guards his spirit against self-centeredness so that he does not become antagonistic or bitter toward her when she expresses her opinions or contributes to his knowledge.

The husband is the representative of God to the home. He should be an initiator and sustainer of the family's spiritual life. The children should learn from his example that it is "manly" to be a Christian husband and father, to read the Bible and pray, to have family devotions, to talk about spiritual values and other issues, to go to church and participate in its activities regularly.

If you are a husband, consider how you can take some steps of growth in banding your home together in a better way for God.

Scriptures for Study

1. *Ephesians 5:21.* What phrase describes the general sensitivity that should exist between believers, including husband and wife, as they relate to each other on a day-to-day basis?

2. *Ephesians 5:23.* What description of the role of a husband is given in this verse?

3. *1 Timothy 3:2–12.* In considering the qualities of potential leaders for the church, identify some key words used to describe the husband's and father's role in the home?

4. *Colossians 3:19.* The Word of God here gives two responsibilities of a husband in his relationship to his wife. What are they? Why do you think this second command is even necessary?

5. *Ephesians 5:28, 33a.* What do these verses say about the love a husband should feel toward his wife?

Additional Study

Look at 1 Corinthians 16:13–14. These verses have five significant applications to husbands and fathers in the home. Use a Bible commentary or other scriptural helps to understand this passage fully. Then complete the chart.

Action Commanded by Paul	Meaning of this Instruction	Practical Insights and Application

Help for the Wife

36

Memorize: Colossians 3:18; 1 Peter 3:1

The role of a wife has been made blurry by two extremes in points of view about the marriage relationship. The traditional, or patriarchal, view is that the woman's place is to be completely in the background as far as decision making is concerned. The other extreme, especially as promoted by the "women's liberation" philosophy, is that the woman should have equal say in all the decisions of the marriage: she has one vote and so does the husband.

The problem, as we see it, is that somehow the team has to function. It cannot function if it has *two* presidents vying for authority. On the other hand, it really isn't a team if the wife is not allowed some input. How do we reconcile these two extremes?

The husband is designated as head of the wife by the Word of God. But that doesn't mean she is of less worth. The apostle Paul gave a good illustration of team function by describing the relationship between God the Father and the Son of God: ". . . the head of every man is Christ, and the head of the woman is man, and the head of Christ is God" (1 Cor. 11:3). The Father and the Son are co-equal, yet they function with the Father as head. The husband and wife are likewise equal *in personal worth,* but in their functioning as a team, someone is designated as the captain—and that is the husband.

As previously mentioned, the wife is the vice-president, or helpmate, which suggests that the "president" (the husband) needs her help. A wife should share her ideas and views freely, even if they are opposite to her husband's stated view. She should always maintain respect for him, however, in the sharing of feelings. If she is not allowed to express herself, she will feel oppressed, which may soon lead to self-hate, bitterness, and depression.

Most decisions in a strong marriage are made together as a result of open and loving communication and sharing. However, what happens if a decision must be made without further delay and the two partners have not found any way to blend their views into a mutually satisfying option? At that point the president must make the decision so that the team can continue to function. This is the point at which the Bible calls upon the wife to voluntarily submit to her husband's leadership. It is "rebellious" for her to insist on the right to have the final word, without the authority to do so.

Submission is her choice as a form of support for her husband. This may ultimately prove that she was right all along, but she never rubs her husband's nose in his mistakes. She supports him and at the same time trusts God to work out his plan through her husband's decisions for the family. This is a matter of faith in God, who told us through Paul: "Now as the church submits to Christ, so also wives should submit to their husbands in everything" (Eph. 5:24).

Is there ever a time when a wife is free to disregard her husband's directives? We believe there are certain exceptions to the rule. A wife may reject her husband's leadership when he demands that she violate a clear statement or command of the Word of God, since her loyalty must first be to God)—or if he becomes physically abusive so that she is in danger of personal harm. Likewise, if remaining with him in an emotionally abusive situation might lead to a mental breakdown, she need not remain subject to his authority. She would need God's special direction in such cases and should carefully seek advice from a pastor or godly professional counselor.

Marriages and families where Christ is the unseen Head are little islands of heaven on earth. Wives, the best way to get your spouse to change is not to demand it, but to set a good example. The most effective approach may be to change your own behavior wherever you can, especially your reaction to things about your husband's personality that irritate you. Communicate your feelings and needs with the underlying message that they do not diminish your unconditional love for him. Give positive reinforcement whenever any positive steps are taken. For best results, stay away from negative messages and demanding mind-sets.

Scriptures for Study

1. *Ephesians 5:22, 24.* What word in these verses describes the proper response of a wife to her husband's leadership?

2. *1 Corinthians 11:3.* By using the functional relationship between the Father and the Son—and we are told that they are equal as members of the Trinity—what does the verse suggest about the worth of the wife, even though her husband is the "head" of the home?

3. *Acts 18:26.* What does this verse tell you about how a husband-and-wife team can be used of God together?

4. *Ephesians 5:33b.* What would be some practical ways a wife could express to her husband the command in this verse?

5. *1 Samuel 15:23.* A person who sets his or her heart in "rebellion" is opening the door to what kind of interference?

6. *Acts 4:18–20.* In what type of situation is one justified in deciding to disobey a figure of authority, thus risking whatever the consequences might be?

Additional Study

Look at 1 Peter 3:1–6. These verses have significant applications to wives (some are negative and some are positive). Use a Bible commentary or other scriptural helps to understand this passage fully. Then complete the chart.

Action Commanded by Peter	Meaning of this Instruction	Practical Insights and Application

Communication in Marriage

37

Memorize: Ephesians 4:15, 4:29

A marriage counselor faces two major tasks: (1) helping the couple to resolve their current conflicts, and (2) helping the couple to develop communication skills so they can resolve further conflicts on their own. In Ephesians 4, the apostle Paul calls all believers to unity. One of the ways this is accomplished is by how they speak to each other. This concept is applicable to marriage and all other personal relationships.

The first principle of good communication that Paul mentions in Ephesians 4 is "speaking the truth in love" (v. 15). Problem communications usually contain only half of this principle and leave out the rest, which is needed for balance. A person may be in the habit of speaking the truth, but not with love. Since this is communicated as a lack of sensitivity and tact, a crude hardness is associated with whatever is said. At the other extreme is the person who speaks loving words, but hides the real truth about his or her real feelings and convictions. Though done in the interest of "love" or not rocking the boat, the truth stays bottled up inside and produces an emotional logjam that blocks honest communication and may result in depression or other disorders.

One of the best ways to speak the truth in love is to share "I feel" messages. A "you" or "why" message can imply blame and call forth defenses on the part of the person with whom you are trying to communicate. An "I feel" message is a personal confession and revelation of who one is and encourages the same type of sharing by the other person.

A practice developed by one of the authors and his wife is to ask each other at the end of each day about the range of emotions experienced that day. For example: "What was your most positive feeling?" "What was your most negative feeling?" The couple then spends some time chatting about that experience and the emotions involved. This kind of exercise enables a personal closeness to be maintained as well as aiding in the expression of feelings, even about stressful situations. This is what speaking the truth in love is all about.

The second principle of communication given by Paul is related to the first and can be summarized as "expressing anger appropriately" (Eph. 4:26). Again, an "I feel" message would be constructive and most likely to lead to a positive resolution. (Review chapter 19 on "anger.") For example: "I felt angry when you broke your word again to our son. Can you help me understand what you feel about this situation?" "Here is what I believe can be done about this matter. What are your feelings?" Kind assertiveness is thereby encouraged, along with an increased opportunity for compromise.

Another principle is "avoiding hurtful words and attitudes" (Eph. 4:29, 31). This tells us to omit anything that communicates temper, put-downs, sharp criticism, and arguing for the sake of arguing. One of the ways the previously mentioned couple practices this principle is to help each other become aware of speech of this type through a warning signal to the offender: "I feel zapped!" The offender thus finds out that something he or she said was offensive and then asks how what was intended could have been said in a more appropriate manner.

Another principle of good communication is "practicing caring words and attitudes" (Eph. 4:32). So much of our speech is matter-of-fact and deals with specific decisions, plans, or problems, but speech is meant to be edifying and nourishing as well. It is a good project in any marriage for each partner to practice expressing compliments and thankfulness for each other's presence.

For example, after a meal, a couple could take the time to express appreciation for some character quality observed in each other recently, giving an example of how it showed. This encourages personal growth. It is also helpful to ask for feedback from each other in such ways as "How have I made you feel accepted lately?" Or "How have I made you feel appreciated lately?" This kind of sharing helps to build intimacy, to contribute to the fulfillment of real needs, and to grow in Christlikeness.

Since good communication takes patience and practice, don't get discouraged by slow progress. Sit down with your marriage partner and make a mutual commitment to learning to express these principles. Then help each other to make them an important part of your day-to-day lives together.

Scriptures for Study

1. *Philippians 4:2–3.* We can assume here that two ladies were at odds. Notice Paul's instructions to his leader-friends on how to communicate to these two believers. Was it a negative threat or a positive suggestion that was to be relayed?

2. *Ephesians 4:15.* Paraphrase in your own words the principle of communication in this verse.

3. *Ephesians 4:26.* Is all anger wrong?

What is the caution connected to this emotion?

What is a good way to be appropriate in speech in carrying out this command?

4. *Ephesians 4:29, 31.* Verse 31 lists some of the unwholesome words and attitudes Paul advised believers to avoid. List them and explain what each one means to you.

5. *Ephesians 4:32.* How would you explain the meaning of the first phrase in this verse to an eleven-year-old child?

How can you translate this attitude into a reality in your style of speech?

Personal Project

The Book of Proverbs has a great deal to say on the subject of the tongue and proper speech. Develop a personal study through this book, using the listed verses and others you find that give insight into the appropriate use of our tongues. (Use the first two passages as examples.)

Proverbs 3:28 (example)

Principle Don't say you are putting something off until tomorrow when you can or should take care of it today.

Application ______________________________

____

Proverbs 4:24 (example)

Principle Separate yourself from unwholesome and dishonest speech.

Application ______

Proverbs 5:2

Principle ______

Application ______

Proverbs 5:3

Principle ______

Application ______

Proverbs 5:4

Principle ______

Application ______

Proverbs ______

Principle ______

Application ______

Proverbs ____________

Principle ____

____

Application ____

____

Proverbs ____________

Principle ____

____

Application ____

____

Proverbs ____________

Principle ____

____

Application ____

____

Handling a Spouse's Infidelity

38

Memorize: Galatians 6:1; 1 Peter 3:8

It is a heartbreaking experience to discover that your spouse has been involved in an affair. It is a crisis time. There is primarily a sense of betrayal, but a wide range of intense emotions will be experienced and should be acknowledged.

Since individuals react differently to a given situation, there is no predictable sequence of feelings about a spouse's infidelity. J. Allen Peterson, in *The Myth of the Greener Grass,* lists five of the most common negative responses that occur before the positive aspects can come into focus:

1. *The Freeze Reaction.* This is a denial of the evidence that the affair is real. Your refusal to confront your partner implies your passive denial, which gives the affair an opportunity to deepen.
2. *The Fry Reaction.* This is an internal burning, characterized by righteous indignation and self-pity. Your self-esteem has been wounded, and you sizzle accordingly.
3. *The Fold Reaction.* You—the injured mate—personalize the affair by taking all the blame and folding into a pile. You dwell on your own past mistakes—some real and some not.
4. *The Fight Reaction.* There is a feeling of rage that could almost kill. Vengeance and retaliation are internal motivations. Since blame is assigned to the other party, ways to punish your spouse are considered. There is also a desire to tear into the third party physically or verbally.
5. *The Force Reaction.* This means pushing hard for an immediate solution, manipulating the people involved for a quick fix.

The truth is that each of these five reactions leads to a dead end. Certainly there is grief when a spouse is unfaithful. The feeling of loss is like a death. In fact, it is worse than a death because of the rejection that seems to be involved. Remember that your life is not ruined and your purpose for living is still in place. (Review chapters on resolving grief, the dangers of unforgiving bitterness, and handling anger constructively in part 2, as well as the previous two chapters in this section.)

Has your spouse repented? He or she probably needs the help of a pastor or Christian counselor to help turn things around. Repentance means a cut-off of all contact with the third party, whether by phone or in person. A "farewell" letter may be in order from your spouse to the third party, saying the affair is over. This should be done with a counselor's assistance and only with your approval of the contents.

Although there is a natural tendency to withdraw from an unfaithful spouse until forgiveness can be granted, it is important that you confront your spouse about his or her adultery. Express your feelings of anger, betrayal, sadness, and grief, but in a way that focuses on what is going on inside your heart. Do not bypass this confrontation and jump prematurely into a token forgiveness that you are not ready to grant. By all means, let God gently lead you to forgive your spouse, but be aware that the pain of the affair may periodically return for up to a year or even longer.

After you have forgiven, commit all thoughts of vengeance to God. Don't punish your spouse by maintaining a wall between the two of you. Most affairs are not based on real love but merely on infatuation, which is actually just a selfish drive for affirmation from another. Consider whether you have failed in some way to satisfy your spouse's needs. If so, make some changes in your behavior.

There is a temptation to ask such questions as "Why did you do it?" "How could you forget all our good years?" "What was he [or she] like in bed?" Don't ask these questions! You may want to write them down and express them to your counselor, but to obsessively bombard your spouse with them will be seen as punishment from you. Remember, judgment belongs to the Lord.

Let the reuniting and healing become an opportunity to grow individually and in the relationship. Seek some good Christian counseling to help you identify the areas of weakness in your marriage. Strive to build a stronger love relationship and a romantic sex life. Deepen your spiritual lives together. Above all, learn how to communicate your feelings and needs more effectively and how to "fight fair." Don't merely go back to the former kind of relationship. Build it into something new and better.

What if the unfaithful spouse does not repent and wants to continue to carry on with the third party? Then you will have to draw the line and say, "No, I will not be a part of that game." You may try to exercise some "tough love" principles at this point, realizing that your spouse's lack of compliance with your wishes may mean that he or she does not want a reconciliation. In that case, after a cooling-off period, separation may be the only acceptable "solution" for both parties, as painful as that may be. Once a marital partner has irrevocably rejected the one-flesh principle ordained by God, that marriage is, in effect, inoperable. At that point, it is important to confer with your counselor or pastor. You will want to consider your options as objectively as possible. It is also important to be constantly aware that God's love and guidance for you will continue.

Scriptures for Study

Hosea, the Old Testament prophet, was married to Gomer, an adulteress who bore "children of unfaithfulness." God symbolically used Hosea's experience in a disastrous marriage to portray Israel's desertion of his own divine leadership. There are guiding principles about handling marital infidelity to be found in this prophetic book. More importantly, there are eternal truths to be learned about God's relationship with his believing children. See what you can discover in the passages listed below.

1. *Hosea 2:1–3.* Here Hosea pleads through Gomer's children for his wife to cease her adultery, implying that otherwise he would "strip her naked" and "slay her with thirst." What principle can we discover in Hosea's words, as they relate to marital infidelity and as they also apply to God's response to *our* unfaithfulness? (*Clue:* Look for figurative meanings.)
2. *Hosea 2:6.* Hosea tells us that he will "block her path with thornbushes . . . so that she cannot find her way." Though the prophet may have meant these threats literally, how might this be accomplished on a psychological level as a means of reconciliation in a marriage troubled by one partner's infidelity?
3. *Hosea 2:7.* What is the expected reaction of an unfaithful spouse to the method cited in verse 6?

4. *Hosea 2:9, 13.* Through his prophet, God foretold bitter consequences for the unfaithful. What "punishment" do you think an adulterous spouse might suffer?

5. *Hosea 2:14–15.* Here God holds out a promise of mercy and reason for hope. How could the "victim" in an adulterous marriage apply this principle to his own efforts toward reconciliation?

6. *Hosea 3:1.* What important command does the prophet receive from God as the proper approach to dealing with his unfaithful wife? (See also 11:8–9, for another way of stating this.)

7. *Hosea 3:2.* We are told that Hosea, as part of the reconciliation process, "bought [Gomer] for fifteen shekels. . . ." Even if he meant this literally, this type of transaction is hardly allowable today. What principle is illustrated here? (*Clue:* Consider the sacrifice and "purchase price" paid so that sinners might be reconciled to God.)

8. *Hosea 3:3.* Here Hosea stipulates a set of rules for his wife, implying his promise to stay with her if she complies. What must Gomer do—specifically and in general—to be assured of Hosea's forgiveness? (Also look at verses 4 and 5 and identify the commitment all believers must make to be assured of the Lord's blessing.)

Additional Studies

Consider the following two passages and list how each could apply to either the person involved in an extramarital affair or the wronged spouse.

Galatians 6:1

____

____

____

Ephesians 4:15

____

____

____

Now see if you can find other biblical passages that relate to this subject. Treat them in the same manner as those listed above.

____

____

____

____

Dealing with Divorce

39

Memorize: Philippians 3:13; 1 John 1:7–9

Divorce is not something people have in mind when they exchange their marriage vows. Yet statistics prove that there are many who eventually say, "I don't believe in divorce, but evidently my spouse does, because—whether I like it or not—here I am as a formerly-married single."

Divorce is somewhat like the death of a spouse. In fact, it can be worse. Although there is a sense of finality to death, there are usually happy memories of the departed one to sustain the bereaved. In a divorce the reminders of the former marriage are largely painful, even when one partner has an unrealistic hope of reconciliation. It is normal to experience the stages of grief reaction after divorce. (Study chapter 24.)

It is very important for your healing that you don't allow yourself to get caught in a guilt trap. True, you may have contributed to the divorce, since there is probably no totally innocent party in any marital breakup. In our humanness, we all fail. But remember that God has provided cleansing for our sins. As we humbly confess our shortcomings, God cleanses and forgives us. So, too, do you need to forgive yourself. Don't continue to punish yourself with self-recriminations. Jesus took all our punishment upon himself.

Accept the fact that you are no longer married! Believe it and begin to act on today's reality. Set aside time for reflection, reading, and meditation. Although the past is gone, you can begin to learn much about yourself by *objectively* considering the mistakes you made during your married years. There are circumstances and people you cannot change, but you can always work on changing yourself. Allow your past and present experiences to help you grow.

Now that you are single, live in the present and look toward the future. Work hard to overcome any anger and bitterness. Persistent feelings of resentment and hostility will spill over and touch everyone close to you, especially your children. Such feelings will rob you of the physical and emotional energy you need to make a new life for yourself.

Assume responsibility for yourself and your own happiness. Seek guidance when necessary, but don't expect others to solve your problems. Stand up and be counted as a whole person. For example, don't let your ex-spouse take advantage of you by reneging on agreements, including child support or visitation arrangements. If this kind of behavior persists, report it to your lawyer immediately.

Realize that your children need both a mother and a father and guard against letting any unresolved hostility deny them this right. Never speak disparagingly of your ex-spouse in front of them. Resist the temptation to throw away all the family pictures that had your ex-spouse in them. It is healthier to help your children keep alive any pleasant memories of the past relationship. After all, those experiences are their roots. Good memories are worth keeping. Finally, don't try to assume both parental roles. It's all right to improve on what you are, but don't try to be what you are not.

Now is a time to make drawing close to the Lord a top priority. This will make a big difference. Read your Bible and pray. Put Christ first in your life and order your life according to biblical priorities. Accept the challenge of getting involved in a Bible-teaching local church. Gain strength and support from small-group activities or Bible studies.

Become active in a Christian singles group, not for the purpose of jumping into a new relationship, but rather to balance out your burdens with loving support, encouragement, and prayers and to add some happy and positive aspects to your life. Be aware that you are especially vulnerable to grabbing on to the false security of a rebound relationship. This decision is usually made in haste and is based on emotion rather than on rational considerations.

Above all, realize that your real security—your sense of being loved and cared for—is found in your relationship to Christ. He promises to meet your needs directly and indirectly through his church or by whatever other means he chooses. God has a plan for you. Leave its workings up to him, as you live one day at a time, trusting him for the strength to endure.

Scriptures for Study

1. *1 John 1:7–9.* According to these verses, is there any sin God does not immediately forgive when we as believers confess it to him?

2. *Philippians 3:13.* How can this verse give sound direction to you if you are recovering from the experience of a divorce?

3. *John 4:16–18.* The woman at the well had been married five times, though we do not know whether some of her former husbands had died or if there were divorces. The matter at hand was her method of rebounding into new relationships. What was the specific issue raised by Jesus?

4. *John 4:10.* What did the Lord Jesus Christ offer to the woman at the well during this mixed-up time in her life? What do those same words say to your heart as a way of finding healing and peace?

5. *Ephesians 2:10.* What does this verse say about God's calling on your life?

Additional Study

Even among godly individuals, disagreement exists on the subject of divorce. Those believers who see one or two justifiable grounds for divorce and remarriage (and not all Bible scholars do) refer to certain passages as allowing—not commanding—divorce. The operative verse is found in Malachi 2:16, where God says, "I hate divorce. . . ." Carefully study the passages listed to develop a personal perspective on this subject.

Genesis 2:24

Significance ____________________

____

Application ____________________

____

Matthew 19:8

Significance ____________________

____

Application ____________________

____

Matthew 19:1–9

Significance ____

____

Application ____

____

Mark 10:1–12

Significance ____

____

Application ____

____

Romans 7:1–3

Significance ____

____

Application ____

____

1 Corinthians 7:12–15

Significance ____

____

Application ____

____

Adjusting to the Death of a Spouse

40

Memorize: Psalm 146:9; Isaiah 54:4–5

The death of any loved one is painful, but perhaps the most devastating grief occurs when it is your spouse who has died. After having shared many years of your life with someone you loved in a "one flesh" union, the sudden loss of that individual produces a loneliness hard to describe. It is normal to experience deep grief and sadness at that time, and the natural progression through the stages of grief should be allowed to take place. (Review chapter 24.)

It is somehow comforting to most people to say good-bye to a loved one through the traditional funeral rituals. Sometimes, at the close of a funeral service, the surviving spouse may wish to take one last look at the earthly home of the loved one and say good-bye out loud. This is almost like a period at the end of a sentence. It does seem to make a difference in accepting the finality of one's loss.

Your children and close friends give their loving support, but you have to determine to rebuild your life and go on living without the loving companionship of your partner. It will not be easy, but there are steps that will make the transition less traumatic.

It is healthy to express your grief with tears, but try to do your crying in the privacy of your home or with a trusted friend who understands. Prolonged and frequent episodes of crying will not be generally well received by casual acquaintances. "Cry and you cry alone," so try to keep a cheerful attitude when you are with others. If you break into tears when old memories come back, your close friends will understand and be supportive, but not if this goes on for years.

If you are angry at God for taking away your loved one, express your feelings of anger to him in a prayer or even by writing God a letter. (Look at Psalm 13:1–4 for an example of how the psalmist did this.) Once those emotions are verbalized, your thinking will become clearer and you will realize that God has not singled you out for punishment.

Since death is a natural part of the life process, you are hardly the only person in the world who has lost a loved one. Many people who have suffered the same loss you have experienced choose to go on with an enjoyable and useful life. Carry on in as normal a way as possible as soon as you can. Return to work or take on some new projects, especially those that involve helping others. Work on your hobbies or start a new one.

Call your pastor and see if there are phone calls or visits you could make to some shut-ins or hospital patients or simply some people who have been absent from church and need a short call of encouragement. Accept invitations from friends who will help you learn to care about living and even laugh again. The key lies in getting out into the world—don't sit around and mope!

It may not be best to immediately sell your home and move to an apartment, even though the home you shared with your deceased mate may seem filled with painful reminders of his or her absence. Find solace in the good memories your home brings to mind. Don't give up on being your own person by becoming someone else's live-in babysitter or housekeeper, thinking this will relieve your loneliness. Usually a year or two will give you enough time to adjust to your new status before making any drastic changes in your lifestyle. Avoid spending useless hours brooding in self-pity. In due time, be available for invitations that may come from appropriate members of the opposite sex with whom you are acquainted.

Do something positive on your own. Be active. Enjoy the public library. Join some clubs. Travel and visit some places you have always wanted to see. Learn to be independent. Enjoy your family's companionship, but don't lean heavily on relatives for your needs. Learn to do the things your mate used to handle. If your car has a problem, call the mechanic. Even if you have never done it before, learn to manage your financial affairs. Master the task of paying the monthly bills. Practice (or learn) some cooking skills, since eating out all the time is expensive.

Remember that God's Word expresses special care and concern for the widowed. The Lord cares for you. Draw close to him and enjoy his presence and grace. Let him love you through your extended family of fellow believers.

Scriptures for Study

1. *Philippians 1:21.* What was the attitude the apostle Paul had toward the possibility of death?

2. *Romans 8:38–39.* In the first part of verse 38 what is the experience that eventually touches each of our lives and that cannot separate us from the wonderful love of God?

3. *1 Thessalonians 4:15–18.* In the middle of verse 17 is the phrase "with them." Who are the people referred to by this phrase? (*Clue:* see verse 13.) What does this passage suggest about a future reunion time?

4. *Acts 16:13–15.* Lydia (verse 14) may have been a widow at this time. Her "household" probably included her employees as well as any older children. As you study these verses, what clues do you see that indicate her desire to get on with her life and to be involved in serving the Lord?

5. *Acts 1:14.* Mary, the mother of the Lord Jesus Christ was probably a widow at this time. What was one of the ministries she pursued as part of her present life?

Additional Studies

Exodus 22:22

Deuteronomy 10:18; 14:29

Job 29:13

Psalms 68:5; 146:9

Proverbs 15:25

Isaiah 1:17

Jeremiah 49:11

Acts 6:1

1 Timothy 5:3–16

James 1:27

Avoiding Co-dependency 41

Memorize: Romans 8:31–32; Philippians 4:13

As Christians we are members of the body of Christ, his church. Although we are individuals with unique and diverse abilities, there is an interdependence that is necessary for the unified body of Christ to function on earth today. We are somewhat dependent on others in almost every area of life, relying on their strengths where we are weak. But the big question is: Where does dependency become a problem?

"Co-dependency" is a term used to describe the attitude and actions of the spouse (and other family members) in relation to a non-functioning member of the family unit, most often an alcoholic. The family, like the church, is a system where each member learns a role in which best to contribute to the functioning of the whole. This system can break down if one member does not pull his (or her) weight. For example, an alcoholic becomes the center of focus as the other family members learn to deny, cover up, and suppress their feelings about the problem, in order to keep the family system intact, at least on the surface. When this happens, everything a co-dependent feels is related to the activities and approval of the significant other—in this case, the alcoholic. (A side effect of this is that the co-dependent actually enables the weaker member to continue in the undesirable behavior.)

Co-dependency usually refers to a dysfunctional (impaired) pattern of living and problem solving that is nurtured by a set of rules within the family system. However, co-dependency can exist even in situations where there is no alcoholic involved. Here are some of the "rules" we set for ourselves, all of which prevent us from operating as a fully functioning individual (as suggested in *Co-dependency,* a book of readings on the subject):

1. It's not okay to talk about problems—instead of, It is good to share my problems and get feedback about myself from others.

2. Feelings should not be expressed openly—instead of, It is good to express any persistent feelings with the appropriate person.
3. I must be strong, right, perfect and make others proud—instead of, I should learn to let go of perfection, details, and the need to be right all the time.
4. I must not ever think of my own interests—instead of, I sometimes need to do things just for me in a healthy, caring way.
5. It's not okay to play; it's important that I not be without something to do—instead of, It's all right to have fun, to laugh, to enjoy and even to be silly sometimes.
6. I must not rock the boat—instead of, I need to face problems and take the risk of healthy change.

One psychiatrist defines dependency as "the inability to experience wholeness or to function adequately without the certainty that one is being actively cared for by another."[1] Dependent people sometimes become love junkies who are so addicted to what they think they need from others that they lose their capacity to give real love and intimacy to others. Dependency is a personality weakness that robs us of self-sufficiency and causes us to lean too strongly on other people.

An approval addict cannot personally turn on the inner light of feeling good about himself unless he has another do it for him. He can endorse himself only when someone he respects approves him first. He actually gives another person the power to control his feelings—to make him feel good or make him feel rejected and worthless.

It is normal to want only positive feedback from our relationships. Worthwhile relationships are protected, however, by recognizing the difference between "wants" and "needs." An individual has a dependency disease or addiction when his dependency on others is on a "need" level. Then his focus is more often on what he should receive, rather than on what he can give to the relationship. Sometimes the dependency is upon another's dependency. In other words, "I need to be needed. I need someone to depend upon me or I cannot feel good about myself."

1. M. Scott Peck, *The Road Less Traveled* (New York: Simon and Schuster, 1978).

The answer to overdependency on another person (or co-dependency) is a stronger dependency on the Lord. Our needs for love and approval are met by God through our relationship to Christ. (Study chapter 29 for more insight on how our basic needs are met.)

We try to teach our counselees to memorize this affirmation: "I choose to take responsibility for my own feelings and behavior." The fact is that no one person or thing outside of our relationship to Christ has the power to make us dysfunctional in our behavior or emotions. Each of us has the spiritual power within us to make the recommended biblical response to any circumstance. We do not need to allow someone else's approval (or the lack of it) to affect us to the point that we become unable to function on our own. Our adequacy is from God.

Scriptures for Study

1. *Romans 8:31–32.* According to verse 31, what is God's disposition toward us, his children? What guarantee of God's commitment to us is given as proof in verse 32?

2. *1 Corinthians 4:3–4.* Why does the apostle Paul show a healthy independence from the disapproval of other people? (Practice saying the first part of verse 3 to your critics so you can keep on functioning with a clear conscience as your self-endorsement.)

3. *Philippians 4:19.* How can you apply this verse to your need for approval and love?

4. *Ephesians 5:18.* To "be filled with the Spirit" means to be fully controlled by the Triune God. How can the truth of this verse, when operational in your life, give you liberty from the emotional control of your life by others?

5. *2 Corinthians 3:5.* How can you use this verse to break the bondage of your dependency upon another person?

6. *Romans 14:8–12.* According to these verses, who is the only one to whom we are accountable?

Additional Study

In 2 Timothy 4, Paul, at the close of his life (v. 6), demonstrates the correct balance between dependency on people and one's ultimate dependency on God. Examine carefully the noted verses, giving the principle shown in Paul's life and a personal application. (Be sure you understand the difference between the interdependence of believers and "co-dependency," as previously defined.)

2 Timothy 4:7–8 (example)

Principle Paul's ultimate goal was the rewards to be received in the presence of God after this life, rather than the temporal rewards of praise and acknowledgment on earth.

Application I am to live life in light of eternity, not simply as controlled by personal or temporal relationships.

2 Timothy 4:9–10

Principle ____

____

____

Application ______________________________________

____

____

2 Timothy 4:11–12

Principle ____

____

Application ______________________________________

____

____

2 Timothy 4:13

Principle ____

____

____

Application ____________________________________

____

____

2 Timothy 4:14–15

Principle ______________________________________

____

____

Application ____________________________________

____

____

2 Timothy 4:16–18

Principle ______________________________________

____

____

Application ____________________________________

____

____

2 Timothy 4:19–20

Principle ______________________________________

____

____

Application ____________________________________

____

____

2 Timothy 4:21–22

Principle ____

____

____

Application ____

____

____

Forgiving Our Parents

42

Memorize: Exodus 20:12; Luke 6:37

You had no vote when it came to choosing who would be the parents who produced the little baby you became. In his sovereignty and for his purposes, God allowed it to work out that way.

Most of us are thankful for the parents we have and the good things that became part of our lives because of them. Yet, we often forget the sacrifices and love that they gave us and remember only where they may have fallen short.

We have all discovered that parents are only human. They have their weakness and hang-ups, which may have been passed down to them from their own parents. Consider the Scripture that speaks of God's "visiting the iniquity of the fathers upon the children unto the third and fourth generation of them that hate me, And shewing mercy unto thousands of them that love me and keep my commandments" (Deut. 5:9–10, KJV). This may well mean that the sinful attitudes and behaviors of parents have a way of being reproduced in the lives of their children and grandchildren, unless one of these turns to God, is saved, and grows in Christ, thus helping to reverse the effects of the negative heritage, which might otherwise continue to be passed on.

The Bible is extremely bold in describing some poor parenting. David was a poor example of morality to his children. Eli, a priest, failed in establishing discipline and boundaries for his children. Many of the wicked kings in the Bible had their identity closely attached to the influence of their parents, although there was no inevitable pattern, just as there is none today. Most of the good kings of Judah are listed as having good mothers and living in Jerusalem. Perhaps that was a winning combination: a godly mother and regular exposure to the temple and the worship of God.

It is easy to blame our parents for our present problems. The fact of the matter is that we have faced a lot of decisions and made many choices in life along the way. If we don't grow out of our problems and make the right choices, it is no one's fault but our own.

One of our choices may be to verbalize the anger we feel toward one or both of our parents for real or imaginary wrongs. This may need to be done, but the best way is through either a loving, face-to-face confrontation or perhaps in a carefully worded letter. When wrongs have been committed, the hurts are real, but we must work through our feelings carefully if we want a healthy and quality life in the future.

Dad may have been away too much and unavailable to you when you were young. Perhaps he deserted the family completely. Maybe he was unaffectionate or even cruel and abusive. Alcoholism may have been a problem for either parent—or affairs, divorce, physical or verbal abuse, perhaps even incest. There may have been rigidity and over-control or the opposite extreme: unconcern or actual abandonment. Although most parents want the very best for their children and try very hard, the possibilities for mistakes are always there, and the results can be devastating. Ineffective parenting may produce painful emotions that can be buried inside for years. This logjam of emotions must become unclogged by verbalizing your feelings in one form or another, if you are to become a fully functional adult. It also opens the way for your parents to tell you their side of the story and communicate their feelings. Perhaps your memory is faulty or you are missing some of the facts.

Then comes the need to forgive. Does God want you to forgive your parents? Yes! He says, "Honor your father and your mother . . . that it may go well with you" (Eph. 6:2–3). Does that mean forgiving them? Yes! Since there are no healthy or spiritual advantages in holding a grudge, it is to *your* advantage to forgive. It is smart; it is wise; it is right—and God commands us to do so.

That doesn't mean you can't make some decisions concerning the quality and extent of your relationship with your parents in the future. It also doesn't mean you should overlook the need to confront them in a kind yet assertive manner if other offenses take place. However, forgiveness and love have tremendous power to motivate change in individuals and in relationships.

Forgiveness is Christlike. Forgiveness means choosing to be a responsible adult. Forgiveness is a way of opening our own lives to the fresh fullness and power of the Holy Spirit. Will you do it?

Scriptures for Study

1. *Romans 8:28.* Do you think this verse may apply to the kind of parents a believer had and the various life-affecting experiences that resulted from their input, whether positive or negative or both?

2. *Psalm 27:10.* What does this verse suggest about the human frailties of our earthly parents?

3. *Ephesians 6:2–3.* What is an important attitude to have toward our parents, even if they seem to have failed us at times?

4. *Acts 16:30–31.* What does the last word in verse 31 suggest about the chances of even an unsaved dad and mom becoming Christians, if we trust Christ and live for him?

Do you think our forgiveness of them would help this goal?

Personal Project

Examine the following passages of Scripture, noting first the teaching presented (as in the first example). Then consider how well your parents applied the principle in dealing with their children, including yourself. (Be specific if you can.) Finally, decide how you, as a parent, will (or would, if you are not yet a parent) apply the guideline to your relationship with your own children.

Passage and Teaching	Did My Parents Follow This Principle?	How Will I Handle My Own Children in This Respect?
***Psalm** 78:5–7* Parents are to teach children God's law		
***Deuteronomy** 6:4–7*		
***Ephesians** 6:1, 4*		
***1 Corinthians** 16:13–14*		
***Proverbs** 23:13–14*		
***Proverbs** 23:15*		
***Proverbs** 23:19*		
***Proverbs** 23:25–26*		

Part 5

Handling Mental, Emotional, and Behavioral Disorders

The last section of this manual will survey disorders that are difficult to overcome without professional counseling. This more technical section summarizes most of the diagnostic categories and disorders listed in the *Diagnostic and Statistical Manual of Mental Disorders* used by psychiatrists, psychologists, and professional counselors. Almost all of these conditions can be improved or even cured, but some are more common, less disabling, and/or easier to treat than others. Among them are a number of general categories.

Psychotic disorders are the most severe. In such disorders, there may be severe disorganization and loss of much contact with reality.

Neurotic disorders are not as severe. Anxiety is their basic characteristic.

Psychosomatic disorders are often linked to repressed anxieties and conflicts. These repressed emotions find physically debilitating modes of expression.

Personality disorders reflect developmental deficiencies. They result from long-standing patterns of overt behavior. Every personality has certain identifiable traits, but when a trait becomes exaggerated to the point that an individual cannot function successfully in daily living, he or she is said to have a personality disorder.

Biochemical conditions are more critical and disabling.

Some research indicates that such conditions as schizophrenia, certain affective (mood) disturbances, and organic mental disorders may have a biochemical basis.

A basic intent for this more technical section is to enable pastors and lay counselors to understand more about specific disorders their counselees may have. It is also intended to be helpful to hospital patients so that they can see that their particular problem is not unique and has been successfully alleviated before. These patients need to receive help and hope through the study of Scriptures pertinent to their condition, as they cooperate with the specific plan of therapy that their professional counselor may prescribe. Thus, this section does not have the practical, do-it-yourself style of the previous sections.

Some applications of Scripture texts to the conditions discussed in this section may seem forced or simplistic to the discriminating reader or the one who has a thorough knowledge of the Scriptures. The authors have found through experience, however, that these texts are of genuine help to people suffering from the disorder under discussion.

It is not as unusual as we may have assumed to find mental or physical disorders within our own social sphere, circle of Christian friends, or even within our own families. As we become more aware of and informed about these disorders, it becomes apparent that everyday people in everyday life suffer from mental and physical disorders. With professional and Christian counseling, support from loved ones, Scripture meditation and memorization, and, in some cases, medical treatment, these conditions can be cured or greatly alleviated.

Mood Disorders

43

Memorize: Psalm 34:4; Psalm 42:5

Mood disorders—also known as affective disorders—are characterized by a disturbance of emotional tone, usually seen as either exaggerated depression or its opposite, intense elation. Some major mood changes occur as an isolated incident, while others last for years or recur periodically.

Bipolar disorder is a term applied to a condition wherein moods of high energy and elation alternate with depression and general blahs. While experiencing a high (or "manic") period, the individual is often cheerful, talkative, and friendly, until frustrated in any way. Then the good humor turns caustic, and a mood change may be triggered. The depressive phase is usually easier to recognize. There is a sad countenance, negative verbalization, perhaps weeping, as well as such physical symptoms as insomnia and loss of appetite. In this phase of the disorder, the individual experiences painful thoughts, anxiety, and delusional thinking that is way out of proportion to the actual events in his or her life.

Depressive symptoms may present themselves without being either preceded or followed by a manic episode. What is called *major depression* has already been described in chapter 22. In treating this disorder, it is important to identify the disturbance as either "single episode" or "recurrent." The former describes a condition in which significant symptoms of depression are present nearly every day for at least two weeks. In the latter situation, the symptoms occur with varying intensity for six months or longer.

A *dysthymic disorder* is characterized by depressive symptoms that manifest themselves over a period of two years or more, yet are not severe enough to be classified as a major depression. Similarly, *cyclothymic disorders* is the term used to describe a condition in which there is a history of alternating high and low moods for at least two years, but the severity or duration of the episodes is not marked enough to diagnose them as "major" disturbances.

Adjustment disorders can also be included in the category of mood disturbances. These occur when an individual's ability to function is significantly impaired because of an identifiable "stressor" (specific situation in life that results in a stress reaction), such as conflicts with other people.

Depending on their severity, most mood disorders can be resolved or at least improved with the help of a Christian-oriented professional trained in psychology or psychiatry. The potential for success of any therapy is dependent in part on the counselee's faith in God and determination to cooperate with those trying to help. For example, mood-changing medication (prescribed by a psychiatrist) is often involved in the treatment of affective disorders; it should be taken faithfully, though only as directed.

Scriptures for Study

1. *Mark 2:17.* According to the Lord's own words, does it show lack of faith to receive help from a physician?
2. *Psalm 42.* What would you say was the psalmist's problem? What one major attitude did he recognize as needed in order to help overcome this?
3. *Mark 3:17.* Analyze the description given James and John in this verse. What kind of emotional energy did they show at times?
4. *Job 30.* Read this chapter from Job, then list some of his symptoms of depression as seen in the following verses:

30:1

30:15

30:17, 19

30:22

30:23

30:28

5. *Job 42:1–10.* Job's life turned around when God led him to change his focus. In these verses, what attitude of Job's was the turning point? What steps can you take to similarly focus your attention, attitudes, goals, and outlook?

Additional Study

Select several verses from the Book of Psalms that you feel will be helpful in counteracting depression or low moods. Give the key thought of the verse plus a practical application.

Verse: ____________

Meaning ____

____

Application ____

____

Verse: ____________

Meaning ____

____

Application ____

____

Verse: ____________

Meaning ____

____

Application ____

____

Verse: ____________

Meaning ____

____

Application ____

____

Verse: ____________

Meaning ____

____

Application ____

____

Verse: ____________

Meaning ____

____

Application ____

____

Verse: ____________

Meaning ____

____

Application ____

____

Verse: ____________

Meaning ____

____

Application ____

____

Schizophrenic Disorders 44

Memorize: 2 Corinthians 12:9–10; Philippians 3:20–21

Individuals with a schizophrenic disorder are out of touch with reality in some marked degree. Their thinking is confused and their verbalization usually rambles from one topic to another, making it impossible for others to follow their train of thought.

These loose or impaired associations reflect an underlying thought disorder caused by a scrambling of neural transmissions, which are normally dependent on a chemical in the brain called dopamine. A dopamine imbalance may be precipitated by too much acute stress in an individual who has a genetic weakness regarding neurotransmitters, or often because of the stress of a difficult early childhood environment.

The underlying thought disorder is reflected in vague, repetitive, stereotyped, or illogical communication. Facts may be obscured or distorted and conclusions reached with inadequate or faulty evidence. Individuals with a schizophrenic disorder generally have a "flat" or inappropriate facial expression, which seems to indicate the nonexistence or distortion of emotions or a decrease in their intensity. For example, an individual may smile or laugh while telling a sad personal experience. Autistic schizophrenics are even more completely caught up in their own world. As fantasies and daydreams increase, such individuals withdraw more and more from their external surroundings.

The emotional ambivalence of a schizophrenic disorder may become so marked that the subject becomes immobilized when faced with the need to make choices. This ambivalence reflects an underlying disturbance of the will, often resulting in loss of motivation and goal-directed activity.

Schizophrenics often experience delusions and hallucinations in the face of solid evidence to the contrary. (A hallucination is hearing, seeing, or feeling things that are not present.) Common types of delusions include those of grandeur (such as believing that you are

Christ or Napoleon) or of persecution (such as thinking that you are being pursued or spied upon or that people are spreading bad rumors about you). Sometimes there are delusions that thoughts are being controlled, inserted into, broadcast from, or withdrawn from one's head.

General schizophrenic indications also include peculiar behavior, poor personal hygiene, eccentric dress, impaired role functioning, and disturbances in motor behavior (mannerisms, grimacing, rigid posture, reduction of spontaneous movements).

A diagnosis of schizophrenia can usually be made only if the symptoms have been present for at least six months. The degree to which the symptoms clear with treatment varies considerably among individuals. Modern medication has brought helpful results to a good percentage of cases. Often an individual can return to near-normal functioning even when some symptoms remain.

Subtypes of these disorders include:

1. *Disorganized* or *hebephrenic* schizophrenia. This type is characterized by an inappropriately silly affect, or emotional mood.
2. *Catatonic* schizophrenia is characterized by psychosomatic disturbances and excitement, and/or by stupor, and a rigid posturing. Mutism is also common in this grouping.
3. *Paranoid* schizophrenia is characterized by delusions of persecutory or grandiose content. Anger may be a prominent feature.
4. *Undifferentiated* schizophrenia is a term used when the symptoms do not fit any of the basic subtypes or when they fit more than one.
5. *Residual* schizophrenia describes a situation in which an individual has had a previous schizophrenia break, is currently not overtly psychotic, but still shows signs of the illness (flat affect, social withdrawal).

Schizophrenia is a pervasive disorder that usually begins in adolescence or early adult life. Since trusting Christ as personal Savior can bring about dramatic changes in some individuals, a Christian psychiatrist can be God's human instrument for bringing about a better quality of life for many schizophrenics. God loves every one of his creatures. Our creator is an all-powerful God who can do the impossible. He is sovereign, which means he might choose to bring healing or impart special grace to help us bear any handicap or burden.

One great consolation for the believer is that our problems are viewed as only temporary when we look at them with eternity in mind. When the Lord Jesus returns, we shall all be changed and receive glorified bodies that will never become physically or mentally sick and never die. In the meantime, our purpose in life is to honor and glorify the Lord with our lives. God's promises and grace give hope to any situation for the believer. This includes ever-increasing information about this disorder and scientific break-throughs in medication that can help reduce the symptoms.

Scriptures for Study

1. *2 Kings 20:1–7.* Hezekiah became seriously ill. What was the first thing he did about his sickness? In examining this passage, can you see the validity of using means such as medication to aid in healing?
2. *James 5:14.* What two steps for healing are suggested in this verse? Since the oil mentioned is "medicinal" according to Bible scholars, what does this step say to you about the use of properly administered medication?
3. *John 9:1–3.* According to verse 3, what is one of the purposes God may have in allowing a person to be sick?
4. *Philippians 3:20–21.* How is our present body described by the apostle Paul? What is in God's absolute plans for each believer in the future?
5. *Revelation 21:4.* What earthly burdens will be missing from our experience someday in heaven?

Additional Study

Examine carefully the apostle Paul's record of his own illness (2 Cor. 12:7–10). Although the weakness he described was probably physical, the same principles can apply to emotional disorders like the ones we have been describing. Note the following observations and give personal insights and applications.

2 Corinthians 12:7a: The purpose of sickness

____

____

2 Corinthians 12:7b: The painful nature of such adversity

____

____

2 Corinthians 12:7c: The effect on the individual experiencing it

____

____

2 Corinthians 12:8: Prayer for recovery

____

____

2 Corinthians 12:9: Principle for enduring

____

____

2 Corinthians 12:9b–10: Proper response

____

____

Paranoid Disorders

45

Memorize: Proverbs 3:25–26; 2 Timothy 1:7

Since paranoid disorders, like schizophrenia, are types of psychoses, individuals so afflicted are in some way out of touch with reality. Some of the symptoms of paranoid disorder are persisent persecutory delusions or delusional jealousy that last at least one week. Paranoid disorders, which occur in one to four percent of the population, prevent effective and appropriate functioning in one's environment, depending on the severity and duration of the delusionary thought system.

The most common subtype is *paranoia,* in which an individual's general thinking pattern is clear and orderly, except for one slice of consciousness that has lost contact with reality. This person may feel spied on, conspired against, followed, drugged, or poisoned. There may be unfounded feelings of jealousy. The delusion tends to become chronic in spite of an accumulation of facts to the contrary. (*Acute paranoid disorder* is the term used when the paranoid symptoms last less than six months.)

Shared paranoid disorder describes a condition in which the individual's delusional system develops as a result of a close friendship with another person (or persons) who has an established paranoid psychotic disorder.

Atypical paranoid disorder (sometimes called *paranoid state*) is a residual category for paranoid disorders not described elsewhere. It is usually a temporary condition, seen most often in individuals who have had sudden changes in their lives or environment (immigrants, refugees, students).

Scriptures for Study

In the life of Job, his so-called friends assumed that fear and anguish had come on him because of his iniquity (Job 4:6). While—in a broad sense—all illness can ultimately be traced to man's sinful nature, it is wrong to assume that an individual's loss of contact with reality is a direct consequence of his or her sin. Yet this is precisely what Job's friends thought (Job 11:14–15). Though there are times when this may be the case, such a direct connection is rarely supported by the facts, at least so far as we humans can determine.

Examine the emotional disorder that afflicted King Saul. Draw observations as to the progression of Saul's mental illness, which in this case is apparently directly related to his rebellion against God. In the verses listed, identify the symptoms of Saul's disorder.

1 Samuel 16:14–17, 23

____

____

1 Samuel 18:1–2

____

____

1 Samuel 18:7–9

____

____

1 Samuel 18:10–12

____

____

1 Samuel 18:15

____

____

1 Samuel 18:17–29

____

____

1 Samuel 19:1

____

____

Continue to trace through 1 Samuel 20:33, listing symptoms that indicate Saul's paranoia about David (include the verse references).

____

____

____

____

Additional Study

Look at Proverbs 3:25 and 2 Timothy 1:7. What do these verses tell us about handling excessive or unreasonable fear?

Anxiety Disorders

46

Memorize: Psalm 118:5–7a; John 14:27

Everyone has fears, apprehensions, concerns, and feelings of insecurity. When appropriate and managed properly, such emotions can protect us from danger or become helpful motivations to think ahead and make plans for handling an anticipated circumstance. However, some fears, apprehensions, and insecurities have little basis in reality and—even if they do—they become a problem if they result in paralysis of action. Anxiety can cause a person to become dysfunctional in his normal responsibilities and relationships of daily life.

Some anxiety disorders are called "phobic disorders." One rather common variety is *agoraphobia,* an irrational fear of leaving the familiar home setting. Agoraphobics may refuse to travel or even to be alone anywhere. They may develop a great deal of anxiety in either closed or wide-open spaces or in crowds of people. The anxiety may become so intense that these individuals experience physical symptoms of panic, such as hyperventilation or rapid heartbeat. Agoraphobics often verbalize a fear that escape might be difficult or help not available in case of sudden incapacitation.

Simple phobia, sometimes referred to as "specific" phobia, is an irrational fear that results in a compelling desire to avoid specific animals, insects, water, and so on. A *social phobia* is an exaggerated fear of social situations, which are seen as a source of humiliation or embarrassment. This might include fears connected with speaking to a group, eating in public, or using public lavatories. Other common phobias include *acrophobia,* which is a dread of heights, and *claustrophobia,* a fear of being in confined places.

Other types of anxiety disorder are called "anxiety states." This category includes *panic disorder.* Individuals so afflicted feel intense apprehension, fearfulness and impending doom, for no apparent reason. Often accompanying these feelings are rapid heartbeat, shortness of breath, dizziness, a fear of dying or of going insane. The fact is that there is no record of a fatality caused by the panic attack itself, but it is certainly an uncomfortable experience.

A *general anxiety disorder* is characterized by chronic, generalized, and persistent anxiety. This often evidences itself by trembling, shaking, or inability to relax. There may also be a pounding heart, sweating, edginess, impatience, or irritability.

The *obsessive-compulsive disorder* also fits under this grouping. Here the individual's most common thoughts are focused on such concerns as contamination, evil people, blaspheming the Holy Spirit, committing the unpardonable sin, or doing violence to someone close. Compulsive actions may include repetitive handwashing, checking, touching, and so on. In this disorder, a person's anxiety is channeled into obsessive thoughts or compulsive actions. Often present is a lack of assurance of salvation, a perfectionistic attitude, and fears about failing, losing one's security, or being disapproved to others. Unresolved guilt or anger issues are usually also present.

Yet another anxiety-related condition is *post-traumatic stress disorder.* Here such symptoms as nightmares, trouble concentrating, guilt, or depression appear after the occurrence of a traumatic event outside the normal range of human experience (for example, an earthquake, flood, car accident). Sometimes the survivor of an accident or natural disaster feels guilty about surviving when others have not. When the symptoms of this disorder continue for six months or more, it is classified as "chronic." If the onset of symptoms is at least six months after the trauma occurs, it is classified as "delayed."

Any of these anxiety disorders is treatable, and the individual can return to a better quality of life. (Other helpful chapters that relate to anxiety disorders are "God Loves You" and "Assurance of Salvation" in Part One; and "Overcoming Anxiety," "Overcoming Guilt," "The Dangers of Unforgiving Bitterness," and "Handling Anger Properly" in Part Two.)

Scriptures for Study

1. *Genesis 15:1.* What solution to fear is mentioned in this verse?
2. *Isaiah 41:10.* What is the key to removing fear, according to this verse?
3. *John 14:27.* What is the source of this peace?

4. *Proverbs 3:23–26.* What was the condition necessary for the fulfillment of the promises given here?

5. *2 Timothy 1:7.* What weapons does God give us to combat our fears?

6. *Philippians 4:6–8.* What two spiritual practices suggested in this passage reduce anxiety?

7. *Isaiah 26:3.* When anxiety dominates our thinking, what would be a good replacement subject?

Personal Project

Select one of the topics listed in the last paragraph of this chapter. Use a concordance or other aids to find at least five verses that speak to this subject. On a separate piece of paper, develop the material in preparation for helping yourself or another person who may experience an anxiety disorder. Include the headings listed below.

Subject

Verses

Meaning

Applications

47 Psychosomatic Disorders

Memorize: Psalm 139:23; 1 Peter 5:6–7

The word *soma* refers to the physical body. In psychosomatic—or somatoform—disorders, there are real physical symptoms of illness without any identifiable organic causes. The symptoms are very real, but they arise from an unconscious transferring of psychological conflicts and anxieties to the body.

These disorders are not to be confused with a condition described as "factitious." The latter is characterized by physical or psychological symptoms that are not genuine; they are actually produced by the individuals and are under their control. Neither should the term *somatoform* disorders be applied to conditions where psychological factors affect the severity of an existing physical condition that has an organic pathology, such as rheumatoid arthritis, or a known pathophysiological process, such as migraine headaches, vomiting, and so on.

Psychosomatic disorders can include a wide range of multiple physical complaints for which there is no organic basis, such as difficulty in swallowing; loss of voice; deafness; blindness; paralysis; diarrhea; painful menstruation; sexual indifference; lack of pleasure during intercourse; pain during intercourse; back or joint pains; chest pain; dizziness.

Conversion disorder conflicts are represented by generally painless physiological symptoms of loss or alteration in functioning, such as blindness, deafness, paralysis, skin disorders, or tics. When psychologically based, these symptoms usually point to an internal conflict or an unacceptable impulse. The symptom may enable the individual to directly avoid some activity that is noxious to him, or it may be a means of gaining more attention or support than he would have received otherwise.

Psychogenic pain disorder is characterized by pain in the absence of a physical finding. Again, the pain itself often allows the individual to avoid some activity that is upsetting to him.

Hypochondriasis is an unrealistic interpretation of physical signs or sensations as "abnormal," leading to preoccupation with the fear of having or developing a serious disease. This term is used when a thorough physical evaluation does not support the existence of an actual disease process that could account for the physical sensations or for the individual's unrealistic interpretation of them.

Finally, *atypical somatoform disorder* is the presentation of imaginary physical symptoms or complaints. Some could include individuals who are preoccupied with some imagined defect in physical appearance, thus does not accurately relate to any actual physical abnormality. Many times such imaginary symptoms are used to cover up spiritual problems that an individual does not want to face.

Most psychosomatic difficulties can be resolved by patient cooperation with a professional Christian counselor. In some cases, such as stress-related ulcers, medication may be suggested as the counseling proceeds. Since these disorders are in the neurosis category, many will relate to resolving of anxieties. You may want to study such related chapters in this book as "Overcoming Anxiety," "Basic Personal Needs," and "Understanding Our Feelings."

Could it be that a few of the people the Lord Jesus cured had disorders like the ones mentioned in this chapter? We cannot know for sure, but it is possible. As God in human flesh, the Son had the power to do anything the Father willed, including raising the dead to life again. However, in some of the recorded miracles, Jesus' method included raising the individual's own faith to a level that would allow the release of mental blocks or conflicts. The main point is that there is special hope for the resolution of any of these disorders. "'According to your faith will it be done to you'" (Matt. 9:29) will begin to mean much more to you, especially if your counseling professional is oriented not only toward the Christian message of salvation but also toward the development of biblical attitudes and behaviors.

Scriptures for Study

1. *Matthew 9:20–22.* In this passage, what was the sick woman's faith-oriented "self-talk," as recorded in verse 21? But what did the Lord Jesus tell her was the key to resolving her disorder?
2. *Matthew 9:27–31.* Do you see any clues in these verses that show the particular responsibility the Lord required of these men in their healing?

3. *1 Peter 5:6–7.* According to verse 6, what is the best attitude we can have when God is dealing with our lives? What is our responsibility in dealing with our anxieties, according to verse 7?

4. *Ephesians 6:16.* What protection do we have from the fearful and hurtful conflicts Satan directs toward us?

5. *Hebrews 11:1.* Some people say that optimism and risk taking based on God's Word are good ways of describing faith. From this verse, do you agree?

Personal Project

Examine carefully in their context the following passages that relate to faith. Write down any insights or practical applications you discover that relate to strengthening your faith or to the role that dependence on God can play in overcoming emotional conflicts of the kind described in this chapter.

Matthew 6:30

____

____

____

Luke 8:25

____

____

____

Luke 8:48

____

____

____

Luke 8:50

____

___

___

Romans 10:17

___

___

___

2 Corinthians 5:7

___

___

___

1 Thessalonians 1:3

___

___

___

Hebrews 11:1

___

___

___

Hebrews 11:6

___

___

___

Hebrews 11:33

___

____

____

Hebrews 13:7

____

____

____

James 1:3

____

____

____

James 2:17

____

____

____

James 5:15

____

____

____

Dissociative Disorders 48

Memorize: Romans 8:37–39; 1 Peter 1:6–7

Dissociative disorders are characterized by alterations in a person's state of consciousness or identity, producing such symptoms as amnesia, sleep walking, or multiple personality.

In *psychogenic amnesia,* individuals become aware that they have a total loss of memory about events covering a period from a few hours to a whole lifetime of experiences. They usually seem alert before and after the amnesia and give no appearance of anything being wrong.

In *psychogenic fugue,* individuals sometimes wander for several days and often far from home, even establishing a new identity. During that time, they have no memory of their past but are unaware that they have forgotten anything. When they return to their former selves, they do not recall the period of time covered by the fugue.

Individuals with a *multiple personality* are alternately dominated by one of two or more distinct personalities. Although many people naively make the assumption that all incidents involving a multiple personality are evil or "demonic," this is not the case. The multiple-personality syndrome often develops as a way of walling off intense pain or conflict, and thus coping. The transition from one personality to another is sudden and often dramatic. Each personality has a complex set of memories that are associated with specific behavior patterns, personal relationships, and attitudes. Often the "primary personality," which characterizes the individual during the greater part of his or her life, is emotionally restricted, moralistic, and proper. The secondary personality, on the other hand, often exhibits dramatically opposite behavior and attitudes.

In a *depersonalization disorder,* a feeling of self-estrangement or unreality is present. Since most people have such feelings on occasion, this diagnosis is rarely made unless the feeling occurs at least six times during a six-week period, with each episode lasting thirty minutes or more.

Finally, *atypical dissociative disorder* is a category used for individuals who appear to have dissociative disorder but do not satisfy the criteria for a specific classification among the types already mentioned. Examples would include the trance-like episodes and prolonged states of identity alterations that occur in persons who have been subjected to periods of extended and intense brainwashing, thought reform, and indoctrination.

The psychological conflicts that lead to dissociative symptoms are often the results of intense disturbances in growth and development that occurred earlier in life. When faced with a situation that arouses excessive grief, despair, or anxiety, many people repress the memory of the disturbing events to get rid of the painful effect. One of the goals of a counselor may be to help restore lost memories to the consciousness. This will enable the person to identify the basic conflict and the possibly erroneous beliefs and conclusions that resulted and to resolve those past conflicts.

Scriptures for Study

1. *Hebrews 11:23–26.* What clues are there in these verses as to the traumatic events experienced as a young child by Moses, that great man of God?
2. *1 Peter 1:6–7.* As mature believers who have experienced various trials in our lives, what is the attitude of faith we should now have as we reflect back? The reason for this attitude is given in verse 7. What positive goal is accomplished in developing the quality of our faith?
3. *2 Corinthians 11:3.* According to this verse, what is the source of the lies brought to our minds, so that our perception of the truth is distorted?

4 *John 15:15.* According to this verse, the Lord Jesus looks on us as his ______, not his servants. What does the Lord do for us as his friends that a master would not do for his servants?

5. *John 15:3.* What effect does learning to think with God's Word as our standard for truth have on us?

Additional Study

In Daniel 4 is described the experiences and recovery process from a serious mental disorder in the life of King Nebuchadnezzar.

Read the entire chapter, then isolate and draw the key thought from the verses noted below. Note especially the ultimate result of the experience, as described in verse 37.

Daniel 4:4

____

____

____

Daniel 4:5

____

____

____

Daniel 4:17

____

____

____

Daniel 4:25–27

____

____

____

Daniel 4:29–30

____

____

____

Daniel 4:33

____

____

____

Daniel 4:34

____

____

____

Daniel 4:36

____

____

____

Daniel 4:37

____

____

____

49 Psychosexual Disorders

Memorize: Proverbs 5:15, 20–21; Hebrews 13:4

This category includes sexual disorders that are the result of psychological rather than structural or hormonal factors. Most psychosexual disorders can be resolved with the guidance of a professional counselor. As with other emotional and behavioral maladjustments, the healing process is expedited when there is a commitment to God—a renewal of the mind through his Word.

Gender identity disorder is characterized by feelings of dislike for one's inborn sexual identity. For example, a *transsexual* wishes to live as a member of the opposite sex. In gender identity disorder of childhood, a young girl will persistently state her desire to be a boy and that she wants to grow up to be a man. She may even insist that she *is* a boy and that she will not develop breasts, has no vagina, and has or will grow a penis. A male with this disorder would state and desire just the reverse. He may be preoccupied with traditionally "female" interests and activities.

Paraphilia is a general term to describe a condition in which sexual arousal occurs in response to objects or situations that are not part of normal patterns of sexuality. This type of disorder is also characterized by gross impairment of affectionate sexual activity between married partners. For example, *fetishism* is a type of paraphilia characterized by the use of undergarments, hair, or other physical objects, as the method of producing sexual excitement. The object so used is often associated with someone whom the individual knew intimately during childhood. *Transvestism* is also a type of paraphilia. It means cross-dressing by heterosexual individuals for the purpose of sexual arousal. Other types of paraphilic behavior include *exhibitionism* (repetitive exposing of one's genitals to an unsuspecting stranger for the purpose of sexual excitement); *voyeurism* (repetitively seeking out situations in which one can "peep" at unsuspecting persons who are naked or disrobing); *sexual masochism* (sexual excitement produced by one's own suffering, such as being beaten, bound, or humiliated); and *sexual sadism* (physical or psychological suffering inflicted on another individual as a method of obtaining sexual excitement).

Homosexuality is a behavior choice made by an individual to practice sex with someone of the same gender. When the term is applied to a male, it usually indicates that the son had an absent or detached father in childhood and spent a great deal of time with his mother. Because of this, he will identify sexually with his mother and even develop her mannerisms. At the same time, he will crave his absent father's affection. In the teenage years, this will frequently result in homosexual temptations. At that point, he can get Christian counseling and spiritual growth to help correct this problem and to resist homosexual urges, or he can choose the homosexual lifestyle that the Bible clearly states is a sinful choice. The temptations are not his fault but are the result primarily of accidental parental mistakes. But yielding to the homosexual tendencies is his own choice. Some men even have multiple heterosexual extra-marital experiences in order to prove to themselves that they do not have some of these homosexual urges.

A *lesbian* is a female who practices sex with another female. She may have developed this bent as a result of having had an absent or workaholic mother and therefore she tends to identify more with her father, since she spent more time with him. She develops his sexual identity and mannerisms and craves her absent mother's affection. She would thus have lesbian tendencies. However, these early childhood influences do not preclude the element of choice in this kind of sexual behavior, because she still has to make a choice whether or not to act out these urges. Gender identity is almost totally the result of parental influence. But choosing to act on these urges is a sin, just as it is a sin for those of us who are heterosexual to act on our extra-marital heterosexual urges.

The term *psychosexual dysfunctions* can take many forms, including *inhibition of sexual desire; inhibited sexual excitement* (including a lack of sexual pleasure and certain bodily changes that normally take place before and during sexual intercourse); *inhibited sexual orgasm* (in either the female or the male); *premature ejaculation; functional dyspareunia* (recurrent and persistent pain during intercourse in either the male or female); and *functional vaginismus* (a recurrent and persistent involuntary spasm of the musculature of the outer third of the vagina that interferes with sexual intercourse.)

Some sexual disorders have their roots in various forms of abuse. Sexual violence or other deviations can be driven by hostility as an underlying dynamic. Past conflicts sometimes produce deep-seated but erroneous beliefs about sexuality that need to be analyzed and corrected. In many cases of sexual disorder, normal sources of security for an individual have become threats and will remain so until the inner conflicts are resolved.

The appropriate expression of sexual love in marriage is from God and is designed as the deepest statement of love between a husband and wife whose hearts are knit together in affection and respect. It is meant to be exciting and satisfying. Marital sexuality is described in the Bible as clean and good, and thus free of inhibitions. The bride in Song of Songs dresses seductively for her husband, teases him, and is aggressive at times. He and she both talk freely about their feelings and about their appreciation of each other sexually. The apostle Paul indicates that marital sex is important as a regular pattern that should not be interrupted except for brief periods by mutual consent, or else Satan will bring extra temptations.

Many forms of so-called sexual deviance are identified as such only if they occur outside the bonds of marriage. Within the marriage relationship, great freedom and creativity in sexual expression is allowed, so long as there is love and respect for the partner's comfort and preferences at all times. Gentleness, compliments, mood-preparing activities, and erotic foreplay are vital to a meaningful and loving sexual experience. When one or both partners have any of the disorders or dysfunctions mentioned previously, counseling for the couple (preferably not just the one partner) is very important.

Scriptures for Study

1. *Hebrews 13:4a.* According to this passage, is "the marriage bed" (marital sex) dirty or clean in God's sight?

2. *Hebrews 13:4b.* Despite the changing moral values of our generation, what is God's will regarding sexual relations outside the marriage relationship?

3. *1 Corinthians 7:2–5.* How does verse 4 relate to the sensitivity of a good spouse to his or her partner's sexual needs? What are *two* commands in verse five?

4. *John 8:1–11.* What was Jesus' attitude toward this penitent woman who had been involved in adultery?

5. *Proverbs 5:15–20.* Note the use of metaphors in the sexual instructions in this passage. What words are used symbolically to command sexual fidelity? What is the recommended way to both overcome temptation and satisfy sexual desires?

Additional Study

Very few Christians have studied Song of Songs (Song of Solomon). Spend some time reading this beautiful poem of love. Then reread it (perhaps aloud with your spouse) and jot down some principles applicable to sexual love in marriage.

Other Psychotic Disorders

50

Memorize: Isaiah 26:3; Philippians 4:7

The term *psychotic* simply denotes a loss of contact with reality, although the symptoms manifested range from hallucinations, delusions, and marked confusion, to exceedingly bizarre behavior. This catch-all category contains several subtypes:

Schizophreniform disorder is identical with *schizophrenia* (see "Schizophrenic Disorders") except that the duration of symptoms is less than six months. It is more likely to have an acute onset and resolution, and tends to have a better prognosis.

Brief reactive psychosis is a diagnosis given if a psychotic episode lasts for less than a week. An overwhelming precipitating stress factor can often be identified. The individual experiences acute emotional turmoil that may include incoherence, delusions, hallucinations, or behavior that is grossly disorganized or catatonic (characterized by physical rigidity or unflexibility, or sometimes excitability).

Atypical psychosis is a residual category to describe psychotic symptoms that do not fall under any of the other broad classifications. For example, symptoms might include a delusion of bodily change without accompanying impairment in functioning, persistent auditory hallucinations, or "postpartum" psychoses.

Schizoaffective disorders are characterized by various admixtures of affective (mood-altering) and schizophrenic-like symptoms (see "Mood Disorders" and "Schizophrenic Disorders"). This diagnosis is used when both types of symptoms co-exist in the patient. An essential requirement for making this diagnosis is that the affective syndrome (manic high or depressive low) must precede or develop concurrently with the schizophrenic-like symptoms—delusions, hallucinations, or loose associations (of thought). In such individuals, suicide is a more common risk than when either type of syndrome exists alone.

Scriptures for Study

Do a study of the uses of the word *mind,* as used in the following passages.

Isaiah 26:3

Meaning ______________________________________

Application ____________________________________

____

Mark 5:15

Meaning ______________________________________

Application ____________________________________

____

1 Corinthians 2:16

Meaning ______________________________________

Application ____________________________________

Philippians 4:7

Meaning ______________________________________

Application ____________________________________

The Paranoid Personality 51

Memorize: Psalm 23:5; Psalm 31:14–15

Exaggerated personality types represent deeply ingrained maladaptive patterns of behaviors that are often present throughout life. These personality disorders are characterized by generalized ways of behaving (perfectionism, suspicion, emotionality), rather than by the clear-cut symptoms (anxiety or depression, for example) that typify so many emotional disorders.

The severity of these behavior patterns fits on a spectrum ranging from a few isolated examples of a particular trait to a full-blown disorder that colors all one's activities. Having a few personality quirks is normal, but when individuals have enough of certain traits to impair their functioning significantly year after year, they can be characterized as "maladjusted." Probably everyone has some of the traits to be discussed in the next two chapters. However, some individuals have enough of the traits of one personality type to be regarded as having a disorder, even though they remain in general contact with reality. Several maladaptive personality types will be discussed in the next seven chapters.

Perhaps the most common maladaptive personality—the paranoid—is suspicious, hypersensitive, argumentative, and jealous, often blaming others for his or her own shortcomings and hostilities. An intense desire to prove their own superiority is the motive behind much of what paranoid personality types undertake. Unconsciously, however, they feel deeply inferior and insecure. Although paranoid types may be highly efficient in what they do, they are too rigid to accept innovations and react with hostility to suggestions and criticism. Although they belittle others, usually to avoid being attacked themselves, their very actions bring about what they try to avoid: further rejection and damage to their self-worth.

Since control is a major issue with paranoid personalities, their insecurities drive them to try to dominate others. This type of person is usually a loner who has few or no close friends and often does not marry. Paranoids who do marry try to control their mates. If their inferiority feelings become too severe, they may gradually lose contact with reality and the disorder may become a full-blown psychosis. (See "Paranoid Disorders.")

Paranoid jealousy is usually based on some objective external factor that is misinterpreted because of feelings of inadequacy, low self-esteem, and ambivalence in one's emotions. Such individuals are constantly watching for confirmation of their jealous delusions in everything said and done around them.

Paranoid eroticism is characterized by both denial of one's own erotic desires and projection of those feelings upon another. For example, a man who has sexual desires for someone may repress those desires yet assign them to the person he desires, convincing himself that *he* is the object of the other person's desire. In this state he might get angry at a woman for being seductive when she isn't being seductive at all. This mechanism allows him to be angry at her for his own sin and feel flattered at the same time.

Paranoid grandiosity seems to parallel a normal phase of childhood development in which children picture themselves as having tremendous powers and abilities. In times of stress and frustration, adults predisposed to paranoid states regress to that early phase and perceive themselves as omnipotent persons whose powers cannot be diminished or denied.

The most frequent and severe type of paranoid personality is *persecutory* in nature. Its chief characteristic is a deep mistrust of others, coupled with an unusually strong tendency to deny one's own hostility and project it onto other people.

A paranoid personality is often the result of lifelong exposure to stressful conditions, such as real or imagined danger or marked discrimination. When met with frustration, threats, rebuffs, loss, or temptation—and having no one to trust or confide in—individuals with this personality type regress to an earlier level or withdraw from their environment. In effect, they are reconstructing reality to confirm their persistent delusions. The anxiety they feel appears to have a real basis in what they perceive as dangerous surroundings. In reality, the origin of that anxiety lies within themselves, but they become uneasy and suspicious and examine their environment distrustfully.

Paranoid personalities sometimes believe they are being subjected to all kinds of tests or that they are targets of contempt by real or imagined persons bent on destroying their reputations or even their lives. Paranoids are most likely to project their irrepressible hostility on authority figures or competitors. The greater their suspicions and misgivings, the less they can depend on anyone but themselves to handle a given situation.

Basic trust in parents or parent substitutes is an essential ingredient in early-childhood development. Without such trust, experiences of frustration, disappointment, and humiliation produce in children a feeling of betrayal and a sense that their environment is hostile. To protect themselves from harm, children may develop a personality that is secretive, critical, insensitive, and hostile. Having never felt trust, they cannot trust others.

Nonpsychotic paranoid personalities are best treated with long-term outpatient psychotherapy by a caring, patient, and well-trained professional. Severe cases are nearly impossible to cure because paranoids are extremely defensive and determined to deceive themselves. Intense hostility causes them to misinterpret any loving attempts to help them.

Treatment of a paranoid patient focuses on two elements: reducing anxiety and reestablishing communication on a realistic level. Certain tranquilizers can often help the patient regain a proper perception of reality. The hurts of the past and the subtle beliefs they produced, the anxiety, and the hostility—all these emotions must be explored in counseling. Grudges must be surrendered to God and forgiveness exercised.

For paranoid individuals, learning to accept themselves leads to learning to accept God and his loving forgiveness. Patients need to realize that God is not like their parents, who might have done a poor job of parenting. By meditating on the Scriptures, it is possible for some patients to accept the fact that God is loving, not hostile. Through their newfound security in God, they can learn to risk trusting others so that their isolation can be permanently broken.

Scriptures for Study

1. *Matthew 7:1–5.* What is the supercritical person forgetting, according to this passage? What should be project number one for this critic?

2. *Romans 2:1.* How does this verse suggest the practice of projection?

3. *1 Peter 2:21–24.* As you examine the last part of verse 23, can you determine the proper alternative to holding a grudge and hoping to personally even the score? What is our calling from God in this regard, according to verse 21?

4. *Psalm 23:5.* How does this encourage your heart to rest in the protection of the Lord and therefore take risks with people?

Additional Study

The Book of Psalms provides one of the greatest resources for overcoming paranoid feelings. Examine the following passages and list your observations, gleaning principles that can help overcome feelings of paranoia.

Psalm 6:7–10

____

____

Psalm 10

____

____

Psalm 27:2–3, 12

____

____

Psalm 31:9–13

____

____.

The Schizotypal Personality

52

Memorize: 2 Corinthians 3:5, Philippians 4:8

The schizotypal personality is characterized by various oddities of thinking, perception, communication, and behavior that are not severe enough to meet the criteria of schizophrenia but can curtail one's enjoyment of life. The "oddities" may include:

1. "Magical thinking," such as superstitiousness, clairvoyance, telepathy
2. Ideas of reference (the feeling that others are constantly talking about you)
3. Social isolation (the individual has no close friends and social contacts are limited to those essential for everyday tasks)
4. Recurrent illusions, including sensing the presence of a person not actually there
5. Odd speech (that which is digressive, vague, overelaborate, or metaphorical)
6. Constructed affect (mood), which may be displayed by an aloof or nonexpressive facial expression that would discourage rapport in face-to-face interaction
7. Paranoid or suspicious fears
8. Hypersensitivity and social anxiety over real or imagined criticism

Scriptures for Study

Since this disorder is so closely intertwined with the thought process, examine carefully the following verses to discover some principles for appropriate and accurate thinking.

Proverbs 23:7

____

___

Romans 12:3

___

___

1 Corinthians 10:12

___

___

Galatians 6:3

___

___

Philippians 4:8

___

___

The Histrionic Personality

53

Memorize: Romans 12:9; 1 Corinthians 9:24–25

Individuals with this personality type can be characterized as theatrical and overly dramatic. Histrionics are highly reactive to people and events around them and intensely expressive of their emotions. These individuals remain "on stage" by such devices as self-dramatization (always drawing attention to themselves), craving for excitement, overreaction to minor events, and angry outbursts or tantrums over the slightest irritation.

Histrionics are also generally characterized by unsatisfactory or impaired interpersonal relationships, and they may be perceived by others as lacking genuineness even if they are superficially warm and charming. These individuals appear self-centered, vain, inconsiderate of others, demanding, dependent, or helpless. They are constantly seeking reassurance and are prone to manipulative suicidal threats, gestures, or attempts.

People with this personality maladjustment tend to be attracted to the opposite sex and are popular socially on a superficial level, since they possess a great deal of charisma. Often there may be a conscious or subconscious seduction of persons of the opposite sex as a result of an unconscious need to prove that the other person is a good-for-nothing like the parent of the opposite sex was, especially if that parent was abusive. Most prostitutes are histrionics. The histrionic is often an outgoing, life-of-the-party individual who radiates excitement, is physically attractive, and desires continual attention. Feelings rather than logic are emphasized in this pattern of behavior.

Some contributing causes of this personality include a background in which love and acceptance were not warmly expressed, especially from a parent of the opposite sex; being overindulged as a child; failing to learn how to think for oneself; getting one's way by pouting or crying; being praised for one's looks rather than for character; and receiving "rewards" by being sick or by threatening to run away as a teenager.

Helpful treatment for individuals whose histrionic behavior is excessive incorporates a reality-oriented approach. People with this personality type need to be encouraged to *think* about what they are doing, especially its effect on others. Responsible behavior should be the primary focus. (For further study, read the chapter on "Understanding Our Feelings").

Scriptures for Study

1. *1 Corinthians 9:24–27.* According to verse 24, anyone who is serious about the Christian life is like a determined athlete. What characteristic is shared by both? In verse 26, what shows that the apostle Paul was no actor? According to verse 27, would you say that Paul followed only the dictates of his feelings?
2. *Galatians 6:4–5.* What does this passage teach that helps a person work his way out of immaturity and dependency?
3. *Matthew 6:16–18.* According to verse 16, what was the underlying motivation of the hypocrites as they fasted?
4. *John 12:42–43.* How can a histrionic "approval addiction" hinder the spiritual life of a true believer, according to this passage?
5. Examine the life of Queen Jezebel, the wife of wicked King Ahab of Israel, by reading 1 Kings 16 through 2 Kings 9. On a separate sheet of paper, list the verses that indicate Jezebel's histrionic personality, including the trait shown and a personal application, if any.

The Narcissistic Personality and the Sociopath

54

Memorize: Proverbs 29:1; Luke 18:14b

The *narcissistic personality* combines many features characteristic of the aforementioned histrionic and the sociopath (see below). For example, narcissistic individuals have a grandiose self-image. They may have an exaggerated sense of importance as related to their achievements and talents or, in some cases, a focus on the unique nature of their problems.

These individuals usually have a preoccupation with success, including fantasies of power, brilliance, beauty, or ideal love. They may be exhibitionistic, requiring constant attention and admiration. Not surprisingly, narcissists often have a problem with criticism, responding with rage or feelings of extreme inferiority, humiliation, or emptiness.

Exaggerated narcissism may show itself on the interpersonal level, since these individuals lack empathy and fail to recognize when others are hurting. They want favors from others but show no responsibility or gratitude in return. Since they often achieve success by taking advantage of others, they tend to alternate between the extremes of over-idealization and devaluation of the people around them.

The *sociopath,* whose behavior can be described as an "antisocial personality disorder," is characterized by repeated conflicts with other members of society. Sociopaths, like narcissists, are extremely self-centered and seemingly unable (or unwilling) to be loyal to individuals, groups, or social values. Selfish, callous, irresponsible, and impulsive, they appear to be incapable of feeling guilt or learning from experience, including punishment. Their failure to follow rules, however, is not a result of ignorance or an intellectual disorder. Sociopaths have an exaggerated tendency to blame others for their actions, thus rationalizing their antisocial behavior.

The development of a sociopathic personality disorder is a lifelong process producing early behavior problems at home and at school and later conflicts with society at large. These antisocial individuals may be just extremely selfish, taking advantage of those around them. Many will regularly engage in a variety of socially unaccepted activities—for example, truancy, drug abuse, burglary, and so on—in contrast to the single criminal action committed by a non-sociopath who makes a serious one-time mistake. Fear of punishment will sometimes cause these individuals to modify their unacceptable behavior, but neither intelligence nor past consequences seem to deter sociopaths from satisfying their immediate impulses. As might be expected, they tend to have poor histories in school and at work.

Sociopaths generally are unwilling to defer pleasure, therefore they often abuse alcohol and drugs in search of immediate gratification. For the same reason they may engage promiscuously in a variety of sexual activities with little emotional involvement. They lack close interpersonal relationships because the give-and-take of intimacy often requires deferring satisfaction or tolerating frustration.

The predominant characteristic of the sociopathic antisocial personality type is the relative absence of anxiety and guilt feelings. It is as if these individuals "harden their hearts" (Heb. 3:8); not feeling guilty means that one has chosen not to feel that way. God's Spirit will continue to strive to impress all people with the need for salvation, but if some willful sociopathic individuals continually reject God's call for repentance, they will eventually reach a point where they will feel relatively free of guilt. Some antisocial personalities do come to know Christ as Savior, however, and become progressively less sociopathic as they mature in Christ.

Two contributing factors to this personality disorder are failure to develop a conscience and a breakdown of the socialization process. For example, children who are repeatedly moved from one foster home to another (or from one boarding school to another) may have difficulty forming the close relationship with a parental figure needed for the development of socially acceptable behavior standards.

Parental inconsistency and hypocrisy can also lead to sociopathic behavior. If parents constantly change the rules or verbally express one set and then act according to another, children learn not to believe in any rules at all. Equally detrimental to normal development are parents who set unreasonable standards and make unrealistic demands. Although many sociopaths come from homes where there is no discipline for rule infractions, others were physically abused (sometimes for no apparent reason) and disciplined to the extreme as children.

In treating this disorder, the counselor must convince the sociopath that each person is responsible for his or her own acts. Precipitating factors never totally excuse a person's antisocial behavior. Sociopaths are helped as they learn to suffer the consequences of their antisocial actions. The purpose of treatment should be the acquisition of a value system or conscience that will allow the development of internal controls for behavior.

When sociopaths trust Christ as Savior, real changes can take place. The new birth results in their receiving a new nature and the indwelling Holy Spirit. The Word of God becomes the standard for values as the new believer grows in the knowledge of Christ. Apart from conversion to Christ, less than five percent of sociopaths ever show any significant improvement, even after prolonged therapy. Recommended reading for the sociopath would be chapters in Part One of this book on "God Loves You," "Assurance of Salvation," "Resisting Temptation," and "Our Struggle from Within."

Scriptures for Study

1. *Proverbs 6:16–19.* According to these verses, which sins are the most detestable to God?
2. *Luke 18:9–14.* In this passage, which of the two men had narcissistic symptoms?
3. *Luke 10:25–37.* What is the commandment stated as an introduction to this parable that repudiates the philosophy of the narcissist? Who in this parable depicts the healthy personality? What people in this parable depict antisocial behavior.
4. *Romans 1:28–32.* What phrase in verse 32 identifies these people as sociopathic? Pick out a phrase from each of the other verses that also shows antisocial behavior.
5. *Luke 19:1–10.* Extrabiblical sources tell us that Roman tax collectors of the first century earned their living only from what extra money, beyond what was owed in taxes, they could manipulate or force taxpayers to pay. What clues in this passage indicate that Zacchaeus was a sociopath? What signs of an awakened conscience

and new spiritual life are noted as a result of Zacchaeus' trusting Christ as his Savior?

6. Examine carefully the life of Judas Iscariot, the disciple who betrayed the Lord Jesus and who was apparently an unconverted sociopath. Look up the biblical references to Judas given below and list antisocial traits or action. Then give the implications for us.

John 12:4–6 ______________________________

Sociopathic action by Judas ______________________

Implications for Us ___________________________

Mark 14:10–11 ____________________________

Sociopathic action by Judas ______________________

Implications for Us ___________________________

55 Borderline, Avoidant, and Dependent Personalities

Memorize: Psalm 118:8; Proverbs 27:17

The characteristic feature of a *borderline personality* is instability in a variety of areas, including extremes in personal relationships. Interaction with others is unstable and intense, with marked shifts in attitude from idealization to devaluation. This type of person characteristically uses manipulation of others as a way of achieving his own ends.

Mood is another unstable aspect of this personality type, and the individual may go very quickly from a normal emotional tone to depression and irritability or lose his temper and be angry much of the time. This individual's behavior is impulsive and self-damaging and may include illicit sex, overspending, drugs, alcohol, gambling, shoplifting, overeating, or self-mutilating acts such as suicide attempts or fighting.

The borderline personality type usually has serious self-image difficulties, especially in the areas of gender identity, career choice, values, long-term goals, and friendship patterns. Not surprisingly, these individuals have an intolerance of being alone and chronic feelings of emptiness or boredom.

The *avoidant personality* is virtually overwhelmed by his or her hypersensitivity to rejection, often reacting with social withdrawal and an unwillingness to enter into relationships unless there are strong guarantees of uncritical acceptance. Such individuals have an intense desire for affection and acceptance, but very low self-esteem. One's actual achievements may be personally devalued, and even minor shortcomings can cause deep discouragement.

People with a *dependent personality* allow others to assume responsibility for decisions in their lives. They tend to subordinate their own needs to those of a supporting person so as to avoid the consequences of making their own choices. Examples of this include allowing a spouse to decide what kind of job one should have or tolerating continual abuse from a spouse. Such individuals have a low level of confidence and often feel stupid and helpless. They also feel intense discomfort when alone and without someone else to lean on.

Scriptures for Study

Examine the following passages of Scripture, developing from them some principles for a balanced relationship with other people: Galatians 6:1–5; Ephesians 4:15–16, 25–32; Proverbs 27:1–17. Use a separate piece of paper if you wish.

The Obsessive-Compulsive Personality

56

Memorize: John 10:27–29; Romans 3:23–24

Obsessive-compulsive people express a low level of warmth to others. They tend to be conventional, serious, and formal. Although such individuals insist that others do things their way, they are usually unaware of the feelings their efforts at control elicit in others. They tend to be workaholics, devoting excessive time and effort to work to the exclusion of personal relationships and pleasure.

Individuals with an obsessive-compulsive personality disorder tend to be self-sacrificing and overly conscientious—perfectionistic workaholics who are frequently quite religious. Many of them are physicians, ministers, lawyers, musicians, engineers, dentists, computer programmers, or other highly trained professionals. The compulsive type is probably more likely than any other to become depressed and has a relatively high suicide rate.

The obsessive-compulsive's perfectionism is fueled by his or her basic insecurity and fear of disapproval. This interferes with the ability to see the whole picture. Instead, the main focus is on details, rules, order, schedules, and lists. Ironically, because of the fear of making mistakes, many obsessive-compulsive-type people often suffer from indecisiveness. As students they have difficulty getting assignments done on time because of frustration over priorities, petty details, or the overly high standards they set for themselves.

Obsessive-compulsive persons feel they need control of their emotions. They try to handle their anxieties about relationships by avoiding intimacy. Often the mechanism used to control their impulses and feelings is to do exactly the opposite of what they would really like to do. For example, a person may carry on a private crusade against sexual promiscuity to counteract the strong sexual desires he (or she) may be repressing. Such defensive action temporarily keeps the individual from having to handle his feelings and perhaps becoming depressed by them. To become suddenly aware of all one's anger, fears, guilt, and sinful desires would be particularly overwhelming for the obsessive-compulsive personality. More than anything, this person wants to be omnipotent and omniscient—to control self, others, and environment—as a reaction to his insecurity and fear of disapproval. To achieve that control, he wants to know every detail about all matters that touch his life.

Obsessive-compulsive personalities usually come from rigid families in which disapproval was forthcoming whenever performance did not measure up to the highest standards. Parental love was perceived as conditional, since most conversation in the home centered around achieving "success" as defined by a parent, neighbors, church leaders, or the community. In this atmosphere of criticism, the grace of God may not have been taught clearly or expressed in daily living. Typical spiritual concerns of obsessive-compulsives are to walk perfectly before the Lord in fear, in order to earn God's acceptance or to maintain his favor on them.

Obsessive-compulsive people often lack an awareness of God's unconditional love and acceptance of them through Christ. They are sometimes overwhelmed with fear that they have committed the "unpardonable sin" (Matt. 12:31–32) or have allowed doubt to enter their mind, thus negating their salvation, healing, blessing, etc. They ruminate over such things as "Do I pray enough?" "Do I believe enough and can I hold on?" "Did I really repent when I came to Christ? Did I pray the right words when I trusted him?" "Am I sincere enough? Am I really convicted by the Holy Spirit?"

Such insecurities cause obsessive-compulsives to look continually for a special sign or word from God instead of taking God's Word at face value. They tend to ignore many easy-to-understand biblical promises about God's grace and eternal security. Instead, they allow a few difficult Scriptures to convince them that their insecurity has some validity.

If you are troubled with disturbing traits of this personality type, read related chapters in this book: "God Loves You," "Assurance of Salvation," "Basic Personal Needs," "Living by Grace," and "Overcoming Anxiety."

Scriptures for Study

1. *John 10:28–29.* What conclusion would even a ten-year-old Sunday-school student reach about the eternal security of the be-

liever after reading these simple promises? (Consider whether difficult passages such as Hebrews 6:4–10—which have no connection to salvation—discount the many simple clear promises regarding the eternal security of the believer.)

2. *Mark 9:21–24.* Can you see the faith yet mixed with doubts expressed by the father of the child in this passage? (We are saved by exercising faith. It is not the strength of our faith that makes the difference, but the strength of our Savior. When you have times of doubt, can you confess this to God with an assurance of his understanding and continual love?)

3. *Romans 3:22–26.* What are the key words in this passage that should assure a believer's heart of eternal salvation? ("Justified" [v. 24] means to be declared righteous by God. This is something that happens when we trust Christ as our personal Savior. It is a declaration by God. It is a new position of eternal acceptance. The ground for our salvation is not the value of our faith but rather the value of the redemption by the blood of Christ. It is not "Did I have faith enough?" but rather "Did Jesus' blood count enough to cancel out the guilt of my sins?")

4. *John 3:16; John 6:35; 1 John 1:7–10.* Is there any sin that is "unpardonable" or that the blood of Jesus Christ cannot cleanse away, according to these verses?

Additional Studies

1. *Read Matthew 12:15–32 carefully.* When this "unpardonable sin" of blasphemy against the Holy Spirit was mentioned by Jesus (vv. 31–32), it was during the culmination of a lengthy and hostile period of unbelief and rejection of Jesus while he was physically present on earth. The reference was not to an occasional or even a long-term lapse of faith sandwiched between periods of trust.

In our experience, those who worry most about having committed the "unpardonable sin" are highly dedicated people who once clearly understood the gospel and trusted Christ completely. However, since they have also had a problem with feeling rejected by at least one parent in childhood, they have transferred that feeling of rejection to their heavenly Father. Once these individuals have learned to work through their feelings of parental rejection, they will find that their worry about having committed the "unpardonable sin" goes away.

Try to detect the answers to the following questions in the above passage in Matthew.

In this unique circumstance, Jesus was physically present among the people of Israel doing miracles by the power of the Holy Spirit. Is he physically present today in the same manner as he was then?

Were the official leaders of Israel stating their criticisms with knowledge of who Jesus was—or were they merely confused and ignorant?

What phrases clearly identify the time periods in which this sin by them would continue its effects?

2. *Read John 16:7–11.* Because some people worry about whether or not they repented enough when they trusted Christ, they ask what repentance really means or wonder if it may be a separate step from believing. But consider why so many Scriptures state "believing" as the *sole condition* for salvation. Because that's what it is! Look at this passage carefully. What is the one sin the Holy Spirit convicts the unsaved person of committing, according to verse 9?

"Repentance" means to have a change of mind. When we trust Christ as our Savior, we have automatically changed our mind about our former attitude of unbelief. We can therefore conclude that repentance and faith in connection to being saved are one and the same thing. One cannot exist without the other. To repent of the sin of unbelief in Christ *is* to believe and depend on him. Thus, to ruminate over whether or not one has felt enough sorrow or remorse is to misunderstand salvation. That attitude focuses on oneself rather than on the person and work of Christ.

57

Passive-Aggressive Personality

Memorize: Matthew 6:14–15; 1 Corinthians 13:4–5

Individuals with this disorder are inwardly aggressive but express their hostile feelings passively. For example, they express anger primarily in subtle, nonverbal ways, rarely openly and in straightforward communication. Although passive-aggressives are deeply resentful at not having their emotional needs met by others, they have learned to become very passive in their response to others, even as they try to accomplish their goals by crafty manipulation. The main symptoms of this disorder surface in these individuals' response to authority, society's demands, or the needs of those with whom there is a close personal relationship.

Obstructionism is one of the behavior patterns exhibited in this personality type. For example, a man married to a passive-aggressive wife might experience her obstructionism in getting to church on time when she is silently angry over something that happened the night before. Sometimes, without doing so on purpose, she may be "unable" to find her lipstick or shoes and, as a result, cause a delay. She may especially tend to use this particular passive-aggressive tactic if her husband is extremely compulsive about being late to church.

Another unconscious way of expressing aggression for this personality type is by pouting and sulkiness. After a disagreement, instead of resolving it maturely, the passive-aggressive person may pout and walk away sullenly. Frequently the only comment will be that "I don't want to talk about it."

Procrastination is another way of letting suppressed anger surface indirectly. A mother who reminds her passive-aggressive son to mow the yard, for example, may find him expressing his resentment by putting off the chore. When he can no longer get by with that, the boy may exhibit another subtle method of expressing aggression, intentional inefficiency. He may cut the grass but deliberately leave unmowed streaks and do a poor job. If he is relieved of the task as a result of his inefficiency, he has learned how to avoid responsibility.

Passive-aggressive traits become exaggerated when a person's dependency needs exceed normal limits for one reason or another, most commonly because of a relationship with an overly domineering parent. Such people have a low tolerance for frustration. Basically insecure, they seek constant reminders that they are loved, but when this unfulfilled need produces anger and depression, they feel very alone. A passive-aggressive style of behavior is often the delayed reaction to the demands of the domineering and controlling parent.

In marital relationships, the passive-aggressive personalities primarily seek their own gratification and may be unwilling to give much to their partner. They share little, including communication about their emotions. When this type of marriage fails, the passive-aggressive may not understand why. The breakup may produce such bitterness and loss of self-esteem that he or she may even contemplate suicide.

Most individuals with passive-aggressive personality disorders could be cured if they come to a point of clearly desiring change and if they genuinely commit their motives to Christ. For further understanding of this disorder, carefully consider the following chapters in this book: "Scripture Meditation and Memorization," "The Dangers of Unforgiving Bitterness," "Handling Anger Properly," "Basic Personal Needs," "Developing a Healthy Self-Concept," and "Communication in Marriage."

Scriptures for Study

1. *Philippians 4:13.* What specific goals of independence and self-sufficiency can this promise help you fulfill within the context of your trust in Christ?

2. *Matthew 6:14–15.* What important step is necessary before we can be assured of daily forgiveness?

3. *1 Corinthians 13:5.* What behaviors connected with passive-aggressiveness are overcome by love, according to this verse?

4. *Ephesians 4:15.* If speaking the truth—but without love—is a deviation from the principle in this verse, what is an opposite way of

violating this principle that may produce an acting out of anger or even depression?

5. *Galatians 2:20.* As you examine this verse, what was the secret to the powerful life of the apostle Paul?

Additional Study

Carefully examine 1 Timothy and 2 Timothy to determine instances in which the apostle Paul sought to discourage even a hint of passive-aggressive (or passive-dependent) personality traits. List the reference, then write out practical applications. Look especially for places where Paul discourages passivity and encourages an active, straightforward approach to our relational lives.

Organic Mental Disorders | 58

Memorize: Galatians 2:20; Philippians 1:21

An organic mental disorder is a temporary or permanent dysfunction of the brain due to a physiological disease process, aging, hormonal imbalance, or the effects of a drug. The organic mental disorders can be generally grouped into five major categories:

1. Delirium and Dementia. *Delirium* is a state of marked confusion that may include disturbance of attention and disordered memory and orientation. Individuals so affected may first lose track of time and then of place. Visual hallucinations are common, with a general increase of these symptoms in the evening, when visual and auditory stimuli are more easily misinterpreted. Delirium is usually the result of alcoholism or drug abuse and is often life-threatening. Delirium should be treated in a hospital setting by both a psychiatrist and an internist or family practice specialist.

Dementia is a progressively severe set of symptoms caused by dysfunction of certain parts of the brain and associated with abnormal and irreversible changes in the brain tissue. The first symptoms are impaired memory, loss of interests, or depression. The patient then develops disorientation, tearfulness, slowed speech, and finally loss of ability to walk or talk. Dementias may develop at almost any age, although *presenile dementia* (before age sixty-five) is less common than *senile dementia* (after age sixty-five). Presenile dementia is often known as Alzheimer's disease. Dementias can sometimes be helped by a psychiatrist or internist carefully selecting medications, but usually not very much can be done to help the demented person. Family therapy by a Christian professional counselor is important, however, to help the remaining family members to adapt and aid the demented family member without suffering from false guilt.

2. Amnestic Syndrome and Organic Hallucinations. *Amnestic syndrome* refers to an impairment in short-term memory, usually related to head trauma, brain infarction (dying or dead sections of tissue), chronic alcohol use, or thiamine deficiency. *Organic halluci-*

nations are traceable to such physiological factors as alcoholism, LSD, sensory deprivation, or seizures.

3. Organic Delusional Syndrome and Organic Affective Syndrome. These two disorders are similar in symptoms to schizophrenia and affective disorders, respectively (see chapters 43 and 48). In the first condition, the delusions are connected to a specific organic factor such as amphetamine, LSD, or marijuana intoxication. *Organic affective syndrome* refers to the disturbance in mood caused by drugs, hormones, steroid medication, Cushing's disease, hyperthyroidism, or some viral illnesses.

4. Organic Personality Syndrome. This condition is characterized by a marked change in personality that has an identifiable physiological basis, such as tremors, trauma, vascular accidents, steroid medication, or thyroid disease. This type of personality change often includes emotional lability (slowness), temper outbursts, sexual indiscretions, marked apathy, or suspicion.

5. Intoxication and Withdrawal. Here, *intoxication* is a general term referring to maladaptive behavior (such as belligerence or impaired judgment) that results from the ingestion or inhalation of a specific substance: alcohol, opioid, barbiturate, cocaine, amphetamine, marijuana, or caffeine, for example. *Withdrawal* symptoms result from the cessation or reduction of a specific substance that was regularly used by the individual to the point of intoxication. The most common symptoms of withdrawal are restlessness, anxiety, irritability, insomnia, and impaired attention. The individual also has a compelling desire to resume taking the substance.

Some of the organically caused disorders listed above are part of a disease process or pattern of aging, both of which are relatively beyond our control. As they grow in their inner lives, believers in Christ can accept aging and deterioration of the physical body as but one stage in the normal life cycle. Even terminal disease and death itself are not so threatening for believers as they look forward to the glories of heaven, to reuniting with loved ones, and especially to meeting the Lord Jesus Christ face to face.

Believers do have control over the power of intoxicants, however. They have the power of the indwelling Holy Spirit, the promises of God's Word, and the support of Christian friends. If you are fighting battles in this area, we encourage you to read the next chapter carefully. Other helpful material in this area includes: "Assurance of

Answered Prayer," How to Gain Meaning in Life," "Building a Christian Support System," and "Living by Grace."

Scriptures for Study

1. *Psalm 90:10.* What is a scriptural fact of life we all have to accept, according to this verse?
2. *Philippians 1:23.* What is mentioned here as a desirable alternative to the apostle Paul's ministry to these people, should that be God's will?
3. *1 Corinthians 6:12.* How could the principle in this verse be used to strengthen our convictions against any enslaving habit?
4. *Galatians 5:19–21.* According to this passage, is drunkenness considered a sin?
5. *Galatians 5:20.* Here, "sorcery," or "witchcraft," is translated from the Greek word *pharmakia,* which refers to worship with the means of drugs. Could this verse be a good basis for rejecting involvement in illicit and/or recreational drugs?

Additional Study

Examine carefully the apostle Paul's perspective on life, adversity, and the future, as expressed in 2 Corinthians 4:7–18. On a separate sheet of paper, list specific verses with practical applications you can discover in them.

Disorders of Substance Use

59

Memorize: Romans 13:14; James 4:7

This term refers to maladaptive behavior patterns associated with the use of certain chemical substances, including alcohol, tobacco, and both illicit and prescription drugs. All of these substances, in varying degrees, are toxic and habit-forming. Unrestricted use of any of them is "abuse" and will eventually be reflected in impaired social or occupational functioning, difficulty in controlling one's use of the substance, and withdrawal symptoms after cessation of use (see previous chapter).

Behavior may be impulsive or irresponsible, with failure to meet important obligations. Personality disorders, such as antisocial behavior, often occur in an individual who has misused either alcohol or drugs. A substance use disorder that begins early in life is often associated with failure to complete school and with low occupational achievement. Traffic accidents and physical injury and illness (malnutrition, hepatitis, septicemia) are common side effects.

These disorders can be divided into two distinct but related phases. *Substance abuse* involves a minimal duration of use for one month, social complications from the use, and psychological dependency. *Substance dependency* implies all of the above plus symptoms of "tolerance" (increasing amounts are required to achieve the desired effect) or "withdrawal" (upon cessation or reduction of the drug). Various types of substance use disorders are associated with the following: alcohol, barbiturates, opioids, cocaine, amphetamines, marijuana, LSD, tobacco.

A large percentage of individuals with this type of disorder have "dependent personalities." They sense an inner inadequacy for which they artificially compensate through the temporary escape provided by an external means. An individual who feels inferior, withdrawn, or depressed may find these symptoms somewhat reduced by leaning on a crutch of substance abuse. Here is a half-person who seeks wholeness in dependency, someone who recognizes that he (or she) is not self-sufficient but knows no better "solution" to his problem.

There is a sense, of course, in which none of us is sufficient in ourselves alone. But, for the believer, God's Word gives the solution: "Do not get drunk [a wrong way to deal with life]. . . . Instead, be filled with the Spirit [the right way to find peace and a sense of adequacy]" (Eph. 5:18). True sufficiency and strength lie in dependence on the power of the indwelling Holy Spirit (2 Cor. 12:9).

Substance abusers sedate their emotional pain through alcohol or drugs, but eventually they learn that the relief is only temporary. These "painkillers" solve no problems. Rather, they add to them by the damage being done to the abuser's body and mind and to the lives of their loved ones. God wants us to be free, not enslaved. God wants us to trust him, not artificial props. Satan is out to steal away life and health, to lie to us by saying, "This practice won't hurt anyone—besides, it will make you feel good." Or "You can't help yourself."

Can this bondage be broken? Yes, it can, but only if you really want the shackles to be removed. It has to start by choosing to turn your life over to Christ. If you have never entered into a personal relationship with Christ, this is your first step. Read carefully chapters 1 and 2 of this book. If you have already trusted Christ as your Savior, come back to him in a fresh dedication and renewed commitment of your life to him.

Next, set up an arrangement with a counselor, pastor, or dedicated Christian friend so that you can have a regular reporting system for your progress. Meet with this person several times a week if possible, for at least one month. Then meet at least once a week for several more months. Make regular phone contacts during this period. Call your friend when you need extra encouragement and prayer. You might also find it helpful to become regularly involved in a support group in which you can both give and receive encouragement with others who share similar struggles. Also read the following chapters in this book over and over as needed: "How to Gain Meaning in Life," "Scripture Meditation and Memorization," "Resisting Temptation," "Our Struggle from Within," "Overcoming Failure," "Developing a Healthy Self-Concept," and "Avoiding Codependency" (especially useful for the family of a substance abuser). Other helpful Minirth-Meier Clinic books include *Taking Control:*

New Hope for Substance Abusers and Their Families (Baker, 1988) and *Helping One Another Change Bad Habits* (Moody, 1987).

Practice this VICTORY plan in your life:

V iew sin as God views it *(1 John 1:9).* Confess it with the attitude of taking God's side against the sin. Then accept God's forgiveness because of the cross, not because you have beaten yourself down long enough to become worthy of it. Practice this part daily, as often during the course of a day as necessary.

I solate yourself from as many sources of temptation as possible. *(Romans 13:14).* Clean your house and work environment of whatever substance you have been abusing. Don't make it easy to yield to temptation. The pressures will come. Don't keep the "stuff" around just in case you get tempted.

Don't stop off at the bars, even to "visit with the gang." Stay away from all unnecessary sources of temptation. The pressures to backslide will be there anyway, but there are certain arrangements you can make in your lifestyle that will reduce them, especially as they affect your leisure time. Be wise in your choices. Don't associate with those who promote and use the substance over which you are seeking victory. You may sympathize with them and want to help them, but the first most important step for you is to help yourself.

C hallenge the devil's temptations with the Word of God *(1 Peter 5:8–9).* James 4:7 says we can put the devil on the run! We have learned from the example of the Lord Jesus Christ that the devil can be resisted by quoting the Word of God.

We learn from the apostle Paul in Ephesians 6:17 that our spiritual weapon against the devil is "the sword of the Spirit, which is the word of God." Therefore, memorize such pertinent Scriptures as Philippians 4:13, 1 Corinthians 6:12, and Ephesians 5:18. Hide these passages in your heart. Then when you feel the temptation recurring, quickly run them through your mind. Since there is power in the Word, you will sense an immediate release from the pressures. You may need to use your weapon again in just a few minutes, but that's all right. If the devil wants to get stuck with the sword of the Spirit again, go ahead and stick him! But be ready to do it by memorizing some key Scriptures.

T rain your mind through positive meditation *(Joshua 1:8).* After having memorized some key verses, take ten minutes in the morning and the evening for at least thirty days, visualizing yourself living out these verses successfully. Add your name to the text as you quote the verse to yourself. Then visualize a scene in which you turn away from temptation and live out the passage you are quoting.

By visualizing yourself turning away and feeling good about experiencing victory, you are mentally rehearsing your obedience. Practice this over and over. Visualize yourself resisting temptation, walking away from it, and feeling good about being victorious. The Word of God promises that you will be successful.

O perate from a position of faith *(1 John 4:4–5).* Accept your position as an "overcomer." You can overcome anything if you are a believer! That is the personal concept that God wants you to accept. Instead of visualizing yourself as a defeated loser who is continually and hopelessly grappling for victory, see yourself in your position in Christ as a winner, enjoying present victory and claiming the top-of-the-hill military advantage in your future encounters with Satan's temptations. In your prayers, thank God for the victory you have one day at a time (or even one hour at a time). Ask him to help you to stand firmly in your place of advantage.

R eckon your renewed self to be dead and unresponsive to the impulses from your sin nature *(Romans 6:11a).* As believers we have an enemy within that is part of our personality. This is called our "old nature," or our "sin nature." It represents our capacity to sin and gives us an instinct for self-centeredness and pride.

Affirm to yourself often each day the accurate personal concept stated in this verse: "I am dead to my sin nature and to my former master, the devil. I am under no further obligation to be any other way but dead to Satan and to sin. I can live in a way that is consistent with the way I am."

Y ield to the Holy Spirit *(Romans 6:11b).* As a believer, your personal concept also includes the fact that you are alive and responsive to God: "I am dead to sin and alive to God. Dear Lord, live your life through me today. Express your love and power through my life, making an impact on others for your glory."

This VICTORY plan will work if you will apply it consistently and purposefully to your life. Victory is experienced one day at a time, according to your dependence upon the Lord. This will be the beginning of a life that frees you from the chains of Satan and gives you the liberty to share this powerful message with others who are going through struggles similar to what you have faced.

Now it's up to you. Jesus said, "Everything is possible for him who believes" (Mark 9:23b).

Scriptures for Study

1. *1 Corinthians 6:10.* From this Scripture, would you conclude that drunkenness is a sin?
2. *Galatians 5:19–21.* The Greek word for "sorcery" in verse 20 is "pharmakia" which means drugs or use of drugs. Would use of illegal drugs or other substance abuse be against the Scriptures?
3. *Revelation 9:21.* In this chapter describing God's future judgment upon the world, what kinds of shackles does Satan have on some people for which even God's judgment does not cause them to repent?
4. *Ephesians 5:18.* Here the word *filled* means "to be controlled." According to this verse, what provision has God given believers to give them sufficiency and adequacy in their spirit, mind, and relationships?
5. *Joshua 1:8–9.* Meditation on God's Word brings success and strength. How is meditation different from merely reading, interpreting, or even memorizing the words?

Personal Project

The Book of Proverbs contains many words of practical wisdom. By either reading through the book or using a concordance, isolate every verse that talks about a "substance" that could be abused.

Verse	Substance	Action to Avoid Substance
4:17	wine of violence	do not drink it

Disorders of Impulse Control

60

Memorize: Romans 6:5–6; James 1:13–15

Certain disorders are distinguished by failure to resist an impulse or temptation to do something that is harmful to the individual or to others. The individual feels a psychological release after committing the act. This category includes several subtypes, as described below.

Pathological gambling is one such uncontrollable impulse. This progressive preoccupation with gambling disrupts one's personal and vocational pursuits and the family's lifestyle and security. Default on debts or arrest for forgery or fraud may ultimately occur. To the Christian, of course, gambling is wrong not only because of the above effects, but because it runs counter to the commandment against covetousness. Excessive reliance on chance expresses one's coveting of another's money without the intention of earning it. It involves seeking to make a quick gain at the implied expense of another.

Kleptomania refers to an impulse to steal objects, usually not for either their monetary value or one's immediate use. Again, the individual feels a release after committing the act. Such thievery is usually done without premeditation or assistance from others. Often connected with this disorder is a love starvation in the individual's childhood that a counselor may want to explore. Moral values may be in place even though there has been a compulsion to steal.

Pyromania refers to an impulse to set fires for the fascination of seeing the flames. This is done with apparent lack of motivation, such as monetary gain or desire to harm others or their property.

Intermittent explosive disorder refers to several recurring episodes of behavior that evidence a loss of control that may result in serious assault upon another person or destruction of property. This behavior is way out of proportion to its immediate cause, which may be a seemingly innocent remark or other neutral incident. An *isolated explosive disorder* is the same as the above, except it describes a single episode of violent behavior.

For a believer, overcoming impulse-control disorders involves not just knowing God's Word but having the power to obey it. To do so, it is vital to yield to the Holy Spirit in every area of one's life on a daily basis. Only in this way is the sin nature that characterizes the old pattern of life put off and the new spiritual nature and godly pattern of life put on in its stead. Instead of focusing on one's emotional deficit and what is not being received from others, there must be a strong focus on one's spiritual surplus. The victory pattern appears when the individual practices a lifestyle of joyful giving—sharing help, service, money, ministry, praise, encouragement, and prayers with others.

True believers learn that the old sin nature is a common source of wrongful impulses. It has the capacity to operate even without the outside temptations from Satan's activities. While there may be psychological dynamics to look at and work through, the pattern of victory must ultimately rest in the spiritual power and control of the indwelling Holy Spirit. Mastery of one's harmful impulses involves self-control, which is described as one part of the fruit of the Holy Spirit (Gal. 5:22–23). We encourage you to study the following chapters in this book for support in this area: "How to Gain Meaning in Life," "Resisting Temptation," "Our Struggle from Within," and "Basic Personal Needs."

Scriptures for Study

1. *James 1:13–15.* Who should we *not* blame for our temptations? Identify the cycle of sin as described in these verses and then name the best point in the cycle for interrupting the flow. What is the difference between "temptation" and "testing" (vv. 2–3)?
2. *Ephesians 4:28.* What new pattern and lifestyle is described in this verse as needed for changing the life of someone who has been a thief?
3. *Philippians 2:13.* According to this verse, when God the Holy Spirit is working in our lives, what *two* elements will be present?
4. *Romans 6:6, 11.* In verse 6, identify the method God has used to enable us to render inoperative the impulses of our sin nature and

its expressions through our body. How does that method translate to our personal daily responsibility, according to verse 11?

Personal Project

One biblical character who evidenced significant struggles in impulse control was Samuel. Examine his life in Judges 13 through 16. On a separate sheet of paper list some passages that illustrate Samuel's loss of self-control and some principles you can discover from these incidents that will help in controlling your impulses.

Eating Disorders

61

Memorize: Romans 6:21; 3 John 2

The recognition of eating disorders has been a relatively modern phenomenon. In 1977 only 4 percent of female teenagers could have been diagnosed with disorders such as anorexia or bulimia. Today, however, a variety of studies indicate that between 15 and 25 percent of females in their mid-teens to mid-twenties suffer from anorexia or bulimia. As many as one-fifth of these sufferers are at risk of dying from their disordered eating behavior.

Anorexia is characterized by an aversion to eating and an obsession with weight loss, even though the mind may be preoccupied with food. *Bulimia* is a related disorder in which the individual repeatedly loses control of eating and goes through cycles of overeating and binging and then purging of the food through vomiting and the use of laxatives. A major factor involved in these disorders is the modern "exercise and diet" message in our society. Slimness, even unhealthy slimness, is "in."

Another factor is today's cultural message to women. Until recently, a woman was seen as fulfilled only as a wife and mother. Physical attractiveness ("to catch a man") was but one aspect of this goal. Then came the unisex decade of the 1960s, followed by the feminist movement of the 1970s. In the 1980s, female dependencies and traditions were replaced by a new insecurity, brought about by conflicts over independence and control, new career opportunities, competition in the workplace, and pressure to succeed professionally. The side effects included unstable relationships, an emphasis on self-assertion, and media campaigns and self-improvement publications that glorified slimness and physical appearance in general.

Bulimia and anorexia have been described as hidden disorders in that those afflicted with the symptoms usually deny their existence, even to family members and doctors. At the start, most bulimics and anorexics are attractive and of normal weight but perceive themselves as overweight and unattractive. People who suffer from eating disorders also tend to suffer from distorted thinking and emotional processes—denial of feelings, looking for magic cures and pat answers to any problem, rigidity, inflexibility, a distorted body image, perfectionism, and, above all, a belief that there is some magic weight that, once attained, will change their lives.

The key component of this type of thinking is "thinness is wellness." There is a powerful desire to control themselves and their weight, coupled with a strong sensitivity to rejection, and a sense of insecurity, which they hate to admit even though it is there. This insecurity is related to the perfectionistic tendencies that often develop out of their need to protect themselves and/or their families from rejection.

Bulimics and anorexics feel intense loneliness, confusion, and anger, which is often traceable to a real or perceived trauma or abuse from childhood. They are easily depressed and apt to feel left out. To maintain trust in a relationship and to know and meet their own needs is extremely difficult for them.

Considering the fact that most anorexics and bulimics carry a burden of distorted truth and ambivalent feelings, it is not hard to understand why they struggle with trusting people and God and even themselves. As might be expected, maintaining relationships is a real problem for them. Since they have distorted the meaning of loving, caring, and protecting in order to fit these concepts into their own lives, these same distortions mar their basic understanding of how God loves, cares, and protects.

Because most individuals with an eating disorder struggle with their ability to maintain an intimate relationship, it is essential that others be involved in the healing process. Proverbs 11:14, 15:22, and 24:6 all advise on the benefit of seeking an abundance of counselors. Overcoming an eating disorder is not a self-help proposition. The support of empathetic, insightful counselors and friends is essential in the process of reinstating healthy life patterns in relating to others, thereby relieving the feelings of loneliness and isolation.

Relief from most disorders comes when one allows oneself to face the sometimes-buried truths in one's life. As painful as this process may be, it is still healthier than trying to live a lie. Jesus says, "Then you will know the truth, and the truth will set you free" (John 8:32). Through sorting out false perceptions and replacing them with the truth of God's love, his Word can begin to take valuable meaning in a person's life.

The major issue for bulimics and anorexics is not food but dealing with a combination of personality traits and underlying emotional issues. This is generally done best in a hospitalized setting. A team approach—including a psychiatrist (an M.D.), a psychologist, a group therapist, a nutritionist, and other related professionals—can help individuals to identify their feelings, become aware of difficulties in relationships, face issues of childhood trauma, and learn to experience and appropriately cope with emotional pain rather than using food as an escape. Usually it is helpful to include the family in the therapy process. A key principle for the bulimic or anorexic is that there is hope.

Even though overcoming an eating disorder is never easy, it can be done. Different counseling techniques are needed for various stages of the disorder. A comprehensive approach, which seeks to integrate all parts of a person—body, soul, and spirit—has the best chance of success.

In his second epistle, Peter said, "His divine power has given us everything we need for life and godliness through our knowledge of him who called us by his own glory and goodness" (2 Peter 1:3). This assures us that God has given us everything necessary for *living* life fully. Anorexics and bulimics are merely *coping* with life. The key comes not just in adding the knowledge of God but in applying that knowledge, whereby we come to a deeper understanding of his truth, which can be an empowering experience indeed!

Scriptures for Study

1. *Proverbs 11:14.* In light of this passage, counseling can make a big difference in the outcome of our problems. Why, or why not, do you think overcoming an eating disorder is a self-help proposition?
2. *Proverbs 15:22.* What varied types of "advisers" would be needed to help someone who suffers from an eating disorder?
3. *1 Corinthians 6:12.* How can we tell if we are taking something to a harmful extreme even though the practice itself is not sinful?
4. *Galatians 5:23.* In this verse, what does Paul mean by "self-control"?
5. *1 Thessalonians 5:14.* According to this verse, with whom are we expected to be patient?

6. *3 John 2.* What does this verse tell us to do regarding our health—and in which *two* areas?

7. *Romans 12:3–5.* How are we to see ourselves in relation to God and to others?

Sleep Disorders | 62

Memorize: Psalm 4:8; John 14:27

Over seventy million people in America suffer from sleep disorders, of which thirty million are estimated to be severe. At least 20 percent suffer for an extended period with insomnia.

During a person's waking hours, the brain works incessantly; it is provided with a rhythmic timing mechanism that requires it to suspend operations slightly after about sixteen hours of continuous activity. The individual who can get by on six or less hours of sleep per night is extremely rare. The person who gets less than four or five hours of sleep per night has a seven-fold increase in his chance of dying at any point in time.

Insufficient sleep often results in a loss of appetite, indigestion, constipation, anemia, and a loss of weight. It may be followed by a lowered resistance to infections and diseases.

Emotional Stresses

Most cases of insomnia are caused by stress. The insomnia, in turn, increases the stress. The primary emotional stresses are either anxiety or depression.

Anxiety, the chief stress involved in insomnia, is usually reflected in difficulty in falling asleep. The anxious individual is in emotional turmoil and feels that something—they're not sure what—must be done. The anxiety may be accompanied by such symptoms as tremor, irritability, rapid heart beat, sweating, being hyperalert, nervous stomach, sighing respiration, or hyperventilation. The anxious person is worried and can't concentrate. (For more information, read chapter 23, "Facing Fears and Anxiety.")

Many individuals cannot sleep because they are afraid that they will not be able to sleep. Fear of not sleeping becomes a habit, producing a conditioned response which keeps the individual awake. When psychiatrists and psychologists tell these people to try to stay awake on purpose for several hours each night, a psychological phenomenon known as *paradoxical intention* occurs, especially in perfectionistic individuals. Most of them will fall asleep rapidly. The minds of perfectionists are constantly involved in obedience-defiance conflicts. As they try to obey their new "command" to stay awake, the defiant part of their personality switches over to fight wakefulness instead of fighting sleep.

Depression, the second major stress involved in insomnia, is often reflected in early morning awakening. The depressed individual usually has no motivation, low energy, and feels blue. (For more information, read chapter 22, "Up From Depression.")

Physical Stresses

Physical stresses of various kinds also play a part in sleep disorders. Chronic physical problems and pain often make sleep difficult. Headaches (caused by such things as anxiety, certain foods, allergies, and physical disease) keep many awake. Specific diseases that often cause sleep problems include thyroid disease, seizures, hypoglycemia, and cerebrovascular disease.

Sleep apnea is a medical disorder that can be caused from a central problem in the brain that shuts off respiration. Sleep apnea also can be caused by a peripheral obstruction of the respiratory tract, which is seen in some individuals who snore. Some snorers may benefit from surgery of the respiratory tract. The medication Vivactil is sometimes prescribed by doctors for individuals suffering from this problem.

Nocturnal myoclonus (involuntary jerking of the legs) keeps some individuals awake. About 20 percent of insomniacs suffer from this.

Restless legs is another mysterious condition that keeps some people awake at night. The legs may tingle, itch, and want to move. A doctor should be consulted for relief from this problem.

A problem somewhat the opposite of insomnia involves hypersomnia—sleeping too much or at inappropriate times. *Narcolepsy* is characterized by daytime sleep attack, catalepsy, hypnagogic hallucinations, and sleep paralysis. The daytime sleep attacks are brief (a few minutes) but can be dangerous since they occur during activity. The catalepsy is a loss of muscle tone that is usually precipitated by strong emotions. The hypnagogic hallucinations usually occur as a person is falling or going to sleep, which can be frightening. Sleep paralysis occurs as a person is falling asleep or awakening. He is fully conscious but cannot move. Medications can often help in narcolepsy.

Night terrors and nightmares involve another category. The nightmares involve frightening dreams with vivid recall. With night terrors, there is intense anxiety and vocalization but not recall since it occurs during a different stage of sleep (stage IV). Psychotherapy may be indicated and medication often helps.

Some other sleep problems include *jactatio capitis nocturna* (head banging), *somniloquism* (sleep talking), *bruxism* (teeth grinding), *somnambulism* (sleep walking), and *enuresis* (bedwetting). With head banging, sleep talking, or sleep walking, a medical doctor or psychiatrist may need to be consulted. Bruxism may need the help of both a dentist and a trained counselor. Bedwetting can be helped by behavior modification techniques and medication.

Stimulants

Caffeine, contained in many beverages and some foods (coffee, tea, sodas, chocolate) can cause wakefulness, especially if much of it is taken near bedtime. Some medicines that may cause wakefulness are ulcer medication, high-blood-pressure medication, and birth-control pills. The nicotine in tobacco is a stimulant that may affect sleep. Amphetamines used purposefully to help a person stay awake can seriously disrupt normal sleep for many days. Exercise near bedtime will cause an adrenalin release, which has a stimulating effect.

Other Causes

Sleep problems may also be caused by sleeping positions, noises and light, and irregular sleeping patterns. Some individuals sleep in awkward positions that may need to be changed. A mattress that is either too soft or too hard may also be a factor. Sleeping on a medium-firm supporting mattress helps many people sleep better. Noises can affect sleep. Contrary to what many people believe, we do not get used to nighttime noises. The bedroom needs to be quiet and with as little light as tolerable. Of course, some children and even adults feel safer with a small nightlight; and the faint sounds of a humming electric fan benefit some people.

How to Get Restful Sleep

Exercise early in the day has both psychological and chemical effects that help people sleep better that night.

L-tryptophan, a precursor of serotonin, the brain chemical that controls sleep, has been called "nature's sleeping pill." It can be found in dairy products, fish, poultry, and meats, and can be purchased in pill form at drug or health food stores. A physician should be consulted regarding its value for particular individuals.

Warm milk and honey, taken just before bedtime, draws blood to the stomach and creates a sleepy sensation by decreasing blood flow to the brain.

A hot bath and massage can help to decrease muscle tension and induce sleep.

No work in the bedroom helps lessen anxiety. Paperwork or other business materials in the bedroom can produce a conditioning response of anxiety.

Techniques for decelerating and resting the mind include the proverbial counting sheep; counting backwards from one hundred to one while imagining yourself writing the numbers on a huge chalkboard; relaxing the muscles one at a time as you imagine a rope or string binding your body and each relaxed muscle loosening the binding from that area. When all muscles have been relaxed—from head to toe—take three slow, deep breaths, becoming increasingly more aware of your breathing. With each exhalation, silently say "sleep," "rest," "peace," "calm," or another one-syllable word, continuing to concentrate on a word as breathing becomes easy and natural.

You can also imagine God's hands or arms as larger than your bed and you lying peacefully in them, as you repeat one of the two following Scripture promises. John 10:27–31 reassures believers that they are eternally secure in God's hands. Deuteronomy 33:27 tells us, "The eternal God is your refuge, and underneath are the everlasting arms."

Listening to or softly singing or humming peaceful music—classical, other "easy listening" music, or well-known hymns—helps soothe and relax many people's minds toward sleep.

Healthy rituals make bedtime an easy-going pleasure. Going through the same activities—personal hygiene, laying out of tomorrow's clothes—night after night, perhaps while humming or singing, condition one to enjoy bedtime as the habitualness of its activities help relaxation. For many married persons, sex has a relaxing effect before sleep.

Regulated air, including fresh-air ventilation with no strong drafts and a temperature of 64° to 69° F., aids sleep.

Physical cures, under a physician's direction, need to be considered for many sleep problems. Also, taking aspirin nightly does help some individuals sleep better, as it relieves physical pain. However, because of side effects to the stomach, a family doctor should help in making this decision.

Avoid drugs and alcohol, which may help one go to sleep initially, but which actually disturb an important part of the productive sleep cycle. Almost all sleeping medications, as well as alcohol, eventually result in tolerance (a need for more and more to produce the desired results, and uncomfortable withdrawal symptoms when taking them is stopped). After one month, almost all sleeping medications are worthless, but may tend to produce psychological addiction. Their effectiveness is built only on short-range use during critical periods. Some over-the-counter sleeping pills can have serious side effects, even psychosis. Alcohol helps one fall asleep faster, but it also causes a person to wake up a few hours later, requiring one or two hours to fall back asleep.

Insight-oriented psychotherapy helps insomnia that is caused or aggravated by anxiety or depression. These symptoms are usually caused from repressed anger and repressed guilt, emotions the insomniac may not even be aware of and which may have depleted the brain chemical serotonin, which is important to a balanced mood and to sleep. A physician, preferably a psychiatrist, can prescribe short-term use of non-addictive, antidepressant medications (which are also sedating) to correct the serotonin imbalance and to produce good sleep faster, while a well-trained Christian psychologist can easily help the insomniac uncover and biblically deal with the repressed anger and guilt. Remedying the anger and guilt will later produce sounder sleep without the aid of antidepressants. Antidepressant medications should never be used unless the person is also receiving psychotherapy.

Troublesome dreams usually involve emotions that are repressed when one is awake, which come out as exaggerated wish fulfillments in the dreams. Dreaming about dying or being harmed personally may involve repressed guilt for which you feel an unconscious need to be punished. Similar dreams about the death of or harm to another person may involve repressed anger toward that person or someone else of the same sex. Praying for insight into such a dream, then dealing with the emotion and problem biblically—involving God's forgiveness, self forgiveness, and/or forgiving the other person—may bring sounder sleep. In some cases, a trained counselor may be needed to help uncover the repressed emotions and events behind the dreams.

Meditation on Scripture, particularly many of the psalms, helps produce a sense of assurance and security as one nears bedtime, particularly when the evening's thoughts may have been disrupted by many disturbances, including reviewing work, family problems, the news of the world, and violent television shows.

(This chapter is taken from *Sweet Dreams: A Guide to Productive Sleep,* by Frank Minirth, et al [Baker 1985].)

Scriptures for Study

1. *Romans 8:35, 37–39.* According to this passage, what can separate us from the love of Christ? In all the perils mentioned here, what are we? How should this affect our ability to sleep?
2. *Matthew 6:34.* What should we do about tomorrow's troubles? Why?
3. *Philippians 4:6, 7.* For what should we be anxious? How do we change anxiety into peace?
4. *Proverbs 3:13–24.* What should we do so that when we lie down we will not be afraid and will have sweet sleep?
5. *Romans 8:1.* What does God do with all things, good and bad? For whom?
6. *Psalm 4:8.* With the Lord, in what do we dwell? When we know and sense this, how will we sleep?

Disorders Seen Early in Life

63

Memorize: Psalm 127:3; Mark 10:15

Some disorders evident in childhood concern mainly the intellect; others involve developmental problems; others, behavioral or emotional problems; and still others center around physical problems. Whether a disorder seen early in life is genetically determined, arises because of a disease process, or is mainly a result of adverse physical or emotional conditions in the child's environment, it is a God-given mandate for us to provide the optimum opportunity for that child to develop to his or her fullest potential.

Mental retardation is a condition in which below-normal intellectual functioning is usually first evident in childhood and is associated with impairment in adaptive behavior. ("Adaptive behavior" is assessed by observing the individual's effectiveness in achieving personal independence and social responsibility appropriate for that individual's age and cultural group.) Roughly 1 to 3 percent of the general population is considered mentally retarded. Certain causative factors can be determined by a physician before a child reaches age two. For some cases, special diets can be used as a treatment or preventative measure in infancy. The subtypes of mental retardation are "mild" (I.Q. level: 50–70), "moderate" (35–49), "severe" (20–34), and "profound" (below 20). "Unspecified retardation" is a term used when the individual is too impaired or too uncooperative to be adequately tested.

Attention deficit disorder is characterized by a short attention span, poor concentration, and distractibility. A learning disability may be an associated feature. The category is divided into two subtypes: with hyperactivity and without it. Children with hyperactivity are impulsive, distractible, disorganized, inattentive, restless, overdemanding, and frequently fail to carry through on a parental or teacher request. Most hyperactivity in children is probably secondary to anxiety and some children outgrow their symptoms at puberty. Professional counseling can be helpful, and—under certain conditions—a psychiatrist may recommend specific medication for the disorder. If a child exhibits this type of behavior to a marked degree and a normal amount of love balanced with discipline is ineffective, parents should have the child tested. Children without hyperactivity in this disorder still have the inattention and impulsivity characteristics.

Conduct disorders are distinguished by persistent antisocial behavior that violates the rights of others. This pattern includes one or more of the following: chronic lying, bullying, abusive language, stealing, vandalism, reckless driving, superficial friendliness based on self-seeking purposes, chronic disobedience, extortion, and breaking-and-entering—all with the absence of guilt feelings. Only if the antisocial behavior occurs before age eighteen does the diagnosis fit into this category of disorders.

Anxiety disorders include three subtypes: *separation disorder,* in which intense anxiety occurs on actual or threatened separation from parents, home, a pet, or school; *avoidant (shyness) disorder,* in which the child avoids strangers to a degree that interferes with peer functioning; and *overanxious disorder,* which refers to generalized anxiety, including excessive worry about the future and about being approved or accepted, especially by authority figures.

Schizoid disorder is another type of maladaptive behavior pattern in children and adolescents. These young people have no close friends. They are reserved, withdrawn, seclusive, self-absorbed, and usually given to frequent daydreaming. Although they may have a preoccupation with obscure topics, they are still in general touch with reality.

Another subtype of dysfunctional behavior in children is the *oppositional disorder.* Here the chief characteristic is demonstrable opposition to parents or teachers. Such youths show continuous argumentativeness, stubbornness, passive resistance, belligerence, lack of response to reasonable persuasion, and provocative behavior.

Elective mutism refers to a child's continuous refusal to speak in school or other social situations. Possible predisposing factors include marital strife in the family or a protective and controlling parent.

Disorders especially characteristic of late adolescence are:

1. *Emancipation disorder*—a conflict that occurs soon after assuming a more independent position relative to one's parents. (Some

adolescents have trouble making decisions and constantly seek parental advice, or—on the other hand—become somewhat paranoid about parental possessiveness.)

2. *Identity disorder*—anxiety and uncertainty about values, friends, career, and goals.
3. *Academic* or *work-inhibition disorder*—anxiety related to school or employment is severe enough to interfere with accomplishing required tasks. (This occurs most often in individuals with a compulsive personality disorder or in families who overly stress achievement.)

Eating disorders (discussed in the previous chapter) encompass a category with four subtypes:

Anorexia nervosa is characterized by an aversion to food that leads to a drastic weight loss greater than 25 percent of the original ("normal") body weight. There is a sense of being fat even when thin, accompanied by an intense fear of becoming obese, both of which emotions underlie a severely reduced food intake. These individuals (usually young women) are often described as having been well-behaved and perfectionistic children.

A second subtype of eating disorder is *bulimia.* This involves recurrent episodes of rapid consumption of a large amount of food in a short period of time. Attempts are then usually made to counteract the binging and thus lose weight by self-induced vomiting, abuse of laxatives or diuretics, and restrictive crash diets. Often connected with either bulimia or anorexia nervosa is a background of rejection, lack of positive reinforcement, a stifling of having fun, unrealistic expectations imposed on them as children, and resultant buried resentment.

Pica is another subtype in this group. This disorder describes persistent eating of nonnutritional substances such as paint, dirt, hair, or cloth. Although there may be an obscure dietary deficiency involved, pica is usually psychologically based.

The last subtype of eating disorder is *rumination.* This is characterized by frequent regurgitation of food without nausea over at least a one-month period.

In a separate category can be listed *stereotyped movement disorders,* identified as either a *tic disorder* or *Tourette's disorder.* The former group might refer to "transient tic disorder." This means that its onset can be during childhood. It shows itself by recurrent, involuntary, repetitive, purposeless motor movements such as twitches of the eye, face, whole head or an entire limb. Duration is at least one month but not more than one year. If the duration is over one year, the diagnosis is "chronic motor tic disorder." "Atypical tic disorder" is a diagnosis made when the tic symptomology cannot be classified in any of the above categories. *Tourette's disorder* is characterized not only by motor tics but also by multiple vocal tics. For example, the child may shout an obscene word over and over. Non-specific brainwave changes may be present in this disorder.

There are several other disorders with physical manifestations, including *enuresis,* in which there is an involuntary voiding of urine, especially at night, to a degree considered "abnormal" for the child's age. *Encopresis* refers to either voluntary or involuntary passage of feces in inappropriate places. It is "primary" if related to developmental delay and "secondary" if related to life stresses.

Stuttering also fits under the category of disorders with physical symptoms. This involves a repetition or prolongation of sounds, syllables, or words. There is often an emotional causative factor present. With proper therapy, recovery occurs in 50 to 80 percent of the children. Medication and/or behavior modification techniques are often helpful.

Sleepwalking disorder is characterized by repeated episodes of sleepwalking in which there is no response to the efforts of another person to communicate. There is also amnesia about the sleepwalking episode.

Sleep-terror disorder is characterized by awaking with a panicky scream and anxiety, with such accompanying manifestations as sweating or rapid breathing.

Pervasive developmental disorder is a defect in acquisition of normal language and social skills.

Infantile autism is characterized by a lack of responsiveness to other human beings that begins before thirty months of age. Autistic children fail to develop normal attachments. As infants they may not "cuddle," and they show an apparent indifference or aversion to affection and physical contact. In early childhood, they fail to develop friendships and also reveal a gross impairment in communication skills. Language is either absent or slow in developing. These children may repeat over and over the same word which has been said to them. The facial expression is inappropriate or flat. Finally, one sees bizarre behavior in general. Autistic children may become very upset if minor changes are made in their environment. They often become fascinated with moving objects and show ritualistic behavior. Predisposing factors to autism include maternal rubella, infantile spasms, encephalitis, and meningitis.

Pervasive development disorders have symptoms that begin after thirty months of age. This category also involves a disturbance in relations with people and an inability to form peer relations. One sees bizarre behavior, extreme irritability over minor events, inappropriate facial affect, peculiar posturing, and speech abnormalities. Self-mutilation, such as head-banging, may be present.

Specific developmental disorder is a catch-all category that includes impairment in reading skills not connected to either inadequate schooling or mental retardation. Associated symptoms may include poor language skills, impaired left-right discrimination, hyperactivity, poor concentration, and so on. *Specific arithmetic disorder* refers to significant impairment in the development of arithmetic skills not related to age, overall I.Q., or poor schooling.

Developmental language disorder includes the failure to acquire any language, acquired language disability, and delayed language acquisition. Failure to acquire any language is almost always a result of mental retardation. Acquired language disabilities are usually the result of disease or trauma. Delayed language acquisition, the most common type of childhood language disorder, can stem from either an inability to express sounds or from an inability to comprehend the sounds of language.

Developmental articulation disorder refers to prolonged "baby talk." Prognosis is good, and only a few such children need professional speech therapy. Such individuals fail to consistently articulate such sounds as *r, sh, th, f, z, l,* or *ch.*

Mixed specific developmental disorder is the diagnosis made when there is more than one specific development disorder but none is dominant. The individual in this category has a mixture of delayed skills impaired to relatively the same degree, such as reading, arithmetic, language, and so on.

Atypical specific language development disorder is a residual category for use when a specific development disorder is not covered in any of the above categories.

Some of the childhood-and-adolescent disorders discussed in this chapter are treatable by medication. Others are improvable through counseling and training. It is important to consult with a psychiatrist, psychologist, or other appropriate specialist when these symptoms are present.

The Lord Jesus especially loves children. During his earthly ministry, they were invited by him to come to him so he could hold them and bless them. There are many mysteries as to why God has seemingly allowed children and other innocents to suffer. Our God of love is not the cause. In times like these, he can meet child and parent in their trial and through his grace impart the strength to bear it. The Lord will lead us out of any difficulty as he wills and draw us to a closer and more intimate knowledge of him. Such questions as why suffering and pain exist will have to wait to be answered when we see him face to face. For now, we must first exercise every possible biblical option and then rest our faith and prayers in divine wisdom and love.

Scriptures for Study

1. *Psalm 127:3.* What is the proper view of our children, according to this verse?
2. *Luke 1:17.* One of God's desires for fathers is described in this verse. What is it?
3. *Luke 1:14–16.* What were the goals to be accomplished in the life of the baby whose birth was predicted in these verses? Which of these goals would you desire for *your* child?
4. *2 Corinthians 12:8–9a.* Instead of healing the apostle Paul in answer to his prayer, what provisions did the Lord make so that Paul could bear his "weakness"?
5. *2 Corinthians 12:9b–10.* What special blessings would be possible for Paul because of his handicap that he could not have otherwise? What was his new attitude toward any weakness or hardships?
6. *Mark 10:13–16.* What attitude did the disciples have about little children wanting to be near the Lord Jesus? What was the Lord's attitude toward these children?

Additional Study

Examine carefully in John 9 the record of the man who was born blind. List by verse the principles in this incident that can be of encouragement both to parents of children with disorders and to the individuals themselves as they grow and develop toward adulthood. Include practical applications if possible.

Verse:

Principle ____

Application ______________________________________

____

Verse:

Principle ____

Application ______________________________________

____

Verse:

Principle ____

Application ______________________________________

____

Verse:

Principle ____

Application ______________________________________

____

Verse:

Principle ____

Application ______________________________________

____

Verse:

Principle ____

Application ______________________________________

____

Verse:

Principle ______________________________

Application ______________________________

____

Bibliography

American Psychiatric Association. *Quick Reference to the Diagnostic Criteria from DSM-III* (The American Psychiatric Association, 1980).

Backus, William. *Telling the Truth to Troubled People* (Minneapolis: Bethany House Publishers, 1985).

Burns, David. *Feeling Good, The New Mood Therapy* (New York: American Library, 1980).

Crabb, Lawrence J., Jr. *Effective Biblical Counseling* (Grand Rapids: Zondervan, 1977).

Crabb, Lawrence J., Jr., *The Marriage Builder* (Grand Rapids: Zondervan, 1982).

Dobson, James. *Hide or Seek* (Old Tappan, NJ: Fleming H. Revell, 1974).

Foster, Timothy. *Called to Counsel* (Nashville: Thomas Nelson Publishers, 1986).

Grunlan, Stephen A. *Marriage and the Family: A Christian Perspective* (Grand Rapids: Zondervan, 1984).

Machir, Virginia H. "Do's and Don't's for Widowhood," *Mature Living* (March 1986).

Meier, Paul and Richard Meier. *Family Foundations* (Grand Rapids: Baker Book House, 1981).

Meier, Paul. *Meditating for Success* (Grand Rapids: Baker Book House, 1985).

Minirth, Frank and Paul Meier, Frank Wichern. *Introduction to Psychology and Counseling* (Grand Rapids: Baker Book House, 1982).

Minirth, Frank and Don Hawkins, Paul Meier, Richard Flournoy, *How to Beat Burnout* (Chicago: Moody Press, 1986).

Minirth, Frank and Paul Meier, Frank Wichern. *Introduction to Psychology and Counseling* (Grand Rapids: Baker Book House, 1982).

Minirth, Frank and Paul Meier, Frank Wichern, Bill Brewer, States Skipper, *The Workaholic and His Family* (Grand Rapids: Baker Book House, 1981).

Narramore, Bruce and Bill Counts. *Freedom from Guilt* (Eugene, OR: Harvest House Publications, 1974).

Peck, M. Scott. *The Road Less Traveled* (NY: Simon and Schuster, 1978).

Peterson, J. Allen, *The Myth of the Greener Grass* (Wheaton: Tyndale House Publishers, 1983).

Richards, Larry and Norm Wakefield. *The Good Life* (Grand Rapids: Zondervan, 1981).

Schuller, Robert H. *Tough-Minded Faith for Tender-Hearted People* (NY: Bantam Books, 1983).

Smoke, Jim. *Growing Through Divorce* (Eugene, OR: Harvest House Publishers, 1976).

Stoop, David. *Self Talk: Key to Personal Growth* (Old Tappan, NJ: Fleming H. Revell, 1982).

U.S. Journal of Drug and Alcohol Dependency and Health Communications, Inc., compiled by, *Co-Dependency An Emerging Issue,* a book of readings from *Focus* on *Family* and Chemical Dependency (Pompano Beach, FL: Health Communications, Inc., 1984).

Wagner, Maurice. *The Sensation of Being Somebody* (Grand Rapids: Zondervan, 1975).